MW01487250

"At a time whe
in the eighties
disappeared, a
gives voice to its hopes and ...
in radically different contexts. Their accounts of discerning how
to reseed a religious life that has been inexorably receding brim
over with energy, creative imagination and unquenchable hope.
The future of the church, as of religious life, is unknowable, but is
all the richer for hearing the honest and courageous voices of the
sisters of today and tomorrow."

— Gemma Simmonds, CJ, director of Religious Life Institute,
Cambridge, UK, and co-author of *God's Call Is Everywhere*

"*Reseeding Religious Life through Global Sisterhood* is an insightful
and beautiful representation of the real experiences of modern
Catholic sisters. This book ought to become required reading for
anyone who is concerned about the shifts occurring in religious
life and curious about what God is creating anew. What a gift to
the church!"

— Julia Walsh, Franciscan Sister of Perpetual Adoration,
Messy Jesus Business podcast host and author of
For Love of the Broken Body

"One of the surest ways to start a new conversation is to ask new
questions. Throughout *Reseeding Religious Life through Global
Sisterhood*, the authors raise new questions that have the potential
to seed new conversations about religious life, particularly as the
US context becomes more beautifully and richly diverse. While
deeply personal in nature, the reflections address universal themes
of identity, purpose, and belonging across generations and
cultures. The authors' vulnerability is an invitation to our own
honesty and depth and reminds us that God is remaking religious
life again through our daily fidelities to grace and circumstance."

— Mary Pellegrino, CSJ, former president of the Leadership
Conference of Women Religious (LCWR)

Reseeding Religious Life through Global Sisterhood

Edited by
Susan Rose Francois, CSJP,
and
Juliet Mousseau, RSCJ

LITURGICAL PRESS
Collegeville, Minnesota

litpress.org

Cover art: *The Parable of the Mustard Seed* by Kelly Latimore. kellylatimoreicons.com. Used with permission.

Library of Congress Cataloging-in-Publication Data

Title: Reseeding religious life through global sisterhood / edited by Susan Rose Francois, CSJP, and Juliet Mousseau, RSCJ.
Description: Collegeville, Minnesota : Liturgical Press, [2024] | Includes bibliographical references. | Summary: "In Reseeding Religious Life through Global Sisterhood, sisters from around the world reflect on a synodal vision and engage in a contemplative dialogue on the emerging future of religious life"— Provided by publisher.
Identifiers: LCCN 2024021441 (print) | LCCN 2024021442 (ebook) | ISBN 9780814689004 (trade paperback) | ISBN 9780814689011 (epub) | ISBN 9780814689684 (pdf)
Subjects: LCSH: Monasticism and religious orders for women— United States—History. | Nuns—United States—History. | Catholic Church—United States—History. | Vatican Council (2nd : 1962–1965 : Basilica di San Pietro in Vaticano)
Classification: LCC BX4220.U6 R48 2024 (print) | LCC BX4220. U6 (ebook) | DDC 271/.90073—dc23/eng/20240821
LC record available at https://lccn.loc.gov/2024021441
LC ebook record available at https://lccn.loc.gov/2024021442

Contents

Introduction

Susan Rose Francois, CSJP,
and Juliet Mousseau, RSCJ

Today, at the beginning of the twenty-first century, religious life finds itself in a reseeding time. The faithful response of today's elder sisters to the call for renewal and adaptation from the Second Vatican Council, during their most generative years, has led us to this moment. We are emerging from a period of expansion, followed by a time of particular charisms, divergence, and pruning, into a change of era marked by the growing awareness of global sisterhood and the common charism of religious life. Even as the structures of large-scale religious life are receding, we are called to risk the bigness of smallness and reseed the next chapter of God's dream for religious life, already present among us.

One way to tell the story of religious life over the centuries is through two of its enduring qualities: constancy and change. God's love is constant, as is the inexplicable urge of individuals and groups to imitate and follow Christ through the countercultural living of the evangelical counsels. What is also constant is the changing state of the human condition lived on earth, our common home, whether it be influenced by ecclesial, economic, environmental, political, scientific, or social realities.

Each generation of religious, therefore, is faced with the complicated calculus of reading the signs of the times to faithfully navigate the intersection of these enduring qualities of constancy and change. The six generations of women living religious life in the Global North today,[1] no matter their age or leadership conference,[2] have lived their entire lives amid this complicated, and sometimes messy, calculus. While the demographics and landscape of religious life in the Global South may look and feel different than in the Global North, it is also part of this dynamic in our increasingly globalized reality.

What is ours to do in this reseeding time?[3] The Spirit is calling us to nurture, cross-pollinate, and graft the seeds already present among us: abundance, charism, connection, diversity, inclusion, and sisterhood. These seeds were planted in our history, and many bore great fruit for the sake of the Gospel. Today these seeds are fragile and vulnerable. They are also strong and vibrant. Both are true in this time of challenge and opportunity.

There is a sense of urgency to this reseeding time. The sacred opportunity for nurturing hope and possibility is necessarily time limited. We must attend to the many and varied needs and responsibilities of this time when the religious life that the present generations have lived is coming

[1] There are six generations in US religious life: Gen Z, Millennial, Generation X, Boomer, Silent, and Greatest.

[2] Two conferences represent US women religious. The Conference of Major Superiors of Women Religious is composed of the major superiors and vicars of 112 communities representing approximately 5,700 sisters. The Leadership Conference of Women Religious has more than 1,200 members who serve in leadership of communities representing approximately 66 percent of US women religious.

[3] Teresa Maya, CCVI, posed this question in her 2018 LCWR presidential address: "Once all the planning is done, we must ask, what is ours to do with the rest of the time? What are we to do with the energy and time we do have, with the collective wisdom among us now?"

to completion. The current generational imbalance in religious life, where communities like ours have a median age of eighty to eighty-three, and approximately 10 percent of women religious are under the age of sixty, necessarily means that an incredible amount of time, energy, and resources is spent on ensuring quality care and quality of life of elder members, as well as tending the legacy and viability of our sponsored ministries, while finding uses for buildings meant for an earlier age. This receding work is important, and it will only speed up and intensify during the next five to ten years.[4]

Equally important is the reseeding work, and this work must not be limited to the periodic critical conversations and discernment processes taking place at the congregation and conference level.[5] Emerging future conversations that do not also tend to the practical conditions necessary to nurture new life, which is already present within large-scale religious life, do a disservice to the future and the present. For example, what are the creative conversations taking place in communities coming to completion, many of which have a *few* younger vowed members, regarding how and where these younger women will live out their call and charism in the next three to four decades of their religious lives? How are we encouraging and supporting the small intercongregational projects and living communities that are being born today of peer connections and in response to the signs of the times, within and across charism families?

---

[4] See National Religious Retirement Office, "2023 Statistical Report." While there are approximately 24,000 women and men religious over the age of seventy in 2023, this number is anticipated to be cut in half to 12,000 by 2033.

[5] LCWR is engaged in a multi-year Discernment of the Future of Religious Life process. https://lcwr.org/resources/discernment-on-the -future-of-religious-life.

We must be vigilant in balancing the reseeding/receding work to avoid inadvertently snuffing out the tender seeds of new life that are emerging through the grace of God and beyond human understanding during this time. We offer two stories from our personal experiences to set the table for this conversation.

Susan – *Jubilees*

I attended my first jubilee celebration as an inquirer. I remember soaking in the joy that exploded all around me, from the blossoms in the floral displays to the smiles on the faces of the sister jubilarians, and the love emanating from the community, family, and friends gathered to celebrate. It was a joint celebration for several sisters celebrating fifty, sixty, and seventy plus years of life as Sisters of St. Joseph of Peace. As a young thirty-something woman contemplating religious life, I was inspired by the commitment these women represented. I was in particular awe of Sister Cecilia Marie Gri, who not only celebrated seventy-five years of religious life that day, but also was chosen by her sister jubilarians to give the homily. It was spectacular.

That first jubilee experience helped me to get over my initial doubts and make the life-changing decision to apply for candidacy, the first stage of initial formation, which I did a few weeks later. "Seeing them, celebrating the jubilees," I wrote in my journal that day in June 2005, "sensing what my life *could be, would be,* makes me know in my core being that this is where I belong." What was it that made me know? Purely and simply, it was the abundant joy I witnessed that day. "My face hurts from smiling and my stomach muscles from laughing," my journal entry continues. "I am never so happy as I am when I celebrate with the CSJPs. The joy is contagious!"

Since that day, I have attended many jubilee celebrations across the congregation. Each celebration mirrors the life, witness, and character of the sister jubilarians themselves. As the median age has increased, so too have the anniversaries of the jubilarians. We rarely celebrate fifty years these days. At one of our recent jubilees, we celebrated Sister Agnes Fox's eighty years as a Sister of St. Joseph of Peace—she was sixteen when she entered! I would have to live to the ripe old age of 112 to reach such a milestone, which I think you will agree is highly unlikely.

In my religious community, we begin celebrating jubilees at twenty-five years, counting from entrance to the novitiate. This means I will not celebrate my first jubilee until the year 2031, just before my fifty-ninth birthday. This also means that many of my sister friends in community—most of whom are thirty or more years older than me—will not be here to celebrate with me and my novitiate classmate or, given likely health or cognitive issues, may not be able to participate in a big raucous celebration in traditional CSJP style. I would be lying if this reality does not make me more than a little bit sad.

The year before my fiftieth birthday I was serving in leadership and living with Sister Sheila Lemieux. One day we were talking about jubilees and we realized that she would be close to ninety by the time my twenty-fifth came around. We joked that I'd need to push her wheelchair to the party. I'm not sure how the conversation reached its destination, but in the end, we decided there was no need to wait to celebrate with my sisters. Sheila promised to throw a big fiftieth birthday party for me instead. True to her word, even though she had moved to the other side of the country after finishing her leadership term while I had been elected to a second term, the next year Sheila returned and hosted not one, but two, fiftieth birthday parties for me with the sisters. In the afternoon we had a lovely tea party with the sisters living in the care center, followed by an evening pizza party with the more active sisters, some of my peers from other religious communities, and my sister and nephew in attendance. Remember that joy that attracted me at my first jubilee? It was overflowing, as was the love. I smile now just thinking about it.

I later overheard my sister Monica telling my brother Michael: "The sisters love Susan! They know her and they *love* her." Just as important as this celebration was for me and my religious sisters, it also planted seeds for my own family to understand my connections with my religious community, more than fifteen years after I entered. Rather than simply lament the high likelihood that many of my sister friends will not be present to celebrate my twenty-fifth jubilee with me, together we reimagined the possibilities and created another space to share our love for community and one another.

My friend Mary Stanco, a Sister of the Humility of Mary, recently celebrated her twenty-fifth jubilee. The liturgy and reception were held in her honor—she was the only jubilarian celebrated that day—and the community chapel in Villa Maria, Pennsylvania, was filled to the brim. One-third of those gathered, sitting on the right, were members of Mary's religious congregation. One third, sitting on the left, were members of Mary's rather large family, including a multitude of nieces and nephews. I was part of the third sitting in the middle of the chapel, friends that Mary had made over the years in other religious communities and through her ministry experiences. We were all there to celebrate God's love manifested through Mary's religious life.

The Gospel passage was Matthew's story of the parable of the sower. I had originally thought that perhaps Mary had chosen the Gospel, but no, it was the reading for the day, and it was perfect. In her reflection on the scriptures, Mary preached about seeds and hope. "In life, there are many challenges that are beyond our control. That is why hope is essential to most gardeners. . . . Imagine, being sown as seeds planted in hope, flourishing and cracking through hard shells, making a journey in darkness to the sunlight continuing to grow and flourish."

Reflecting on her twenty-five years as a woman religious, Mary spoke of her hopes for religious life in this time. "To live fully as a religious at this time in history is a recognition that what once was is no longer. . . . God is faithful. In the face of a chaotic world, changes in the church, and a volatile society, we are still here. Together we figure out where religious life is going and do the best we can to respond with courage, faith, and hope. We are still here. Love brings about justice and peace. Much has been done by many religious women over the years and we celebrate the legacy. And there are sisters who continue to strive to respond to the Gospel call in the world we find ourselves in today. WE. ARE. HERE."[6]

I had not talked to Mary about this book project prior to her jubilee. And yet, her powerful reflection on her jubilee day mirrors the hopes and dreams embodied in this book project. That, my friends, says to me, that the Spirit is moving. Are we listening?

Juliet – *Life from Fire*

Kenwood was a storied place in the Society of the Sacred Heart. A fortress of a convent in the trees of Albany, New York, it was the noviceship for the majority of the Society's history in North America, from 1864 to 1969. Generations

---

[6] Mary Stanco, "25th Jubilee Reflection" (Homily, jubilee liturgy of the Sisters of the Humility of Mary, July 15, 2023).

of sisters had fond or not-so-fond memories of their first introduction to religious life at Kenwood.

By the time I arrived at Kenwood as a discerning woman, it was no longer the noviceship. In fact, it was mostly vacant and the few remaining sisters were soon to move out. The occasion was the last event that the Religious of the Sacred Heart of Jesus were to have there, an eight-day retreat on Sacred Heart spirituality that was primarily for the local RSCJ retirement community and secondarily for a handful of others—including three "IWs" (Interested Women) and the vocations director. It was a sort of farewell, with hints of that theme emerging throughout the retreat. The retirement community moved in 2008, and the building was completely empty starting in 2009. The farewell of the sisters moving out was followed by another farewell, when the building was sold in 2017.

My first experience at Kenwood was also my last. It was marked by a sense of what was past—a beautiful old building that was nearly empty. The IWs and the vocation director stayed in a separate wing, which used to be where novices lived. We were in a small corner on the fourth floor, near a walkway connected to the other building. Only our little corner of that building was occupied. While full of stories, the empty rooms and dusty walls also spoke of a quiet fading into history.

Though I was struck by the emptiness of the building, I was also drawn to the love of the sisters. I remember watching as they cared for one another and listening to their stories of life, teaching, prayer, and aging. I was drawn into the Sacred Heart and the journey of life, as we sang "Jerusalem, My Destiny" and prayed with Jesus' life story and love for humanity.

In the fifteen years that have passed since that retreat, religious life has become fundamental to my self-understanding and even to my ministerial commitments. My formation, though it was very different from the Kenwood novitiate plan, steeped me in the spirituality of Jesus' Sacred Heart, love for prayer and community life, and the call to listen to the needs of the world around me and respond according to my gifts. While Kenwood's novitiate classes approached a hundred sisters at their height, my class of one trained me in the enduring values and priorities that my elder sisters learned in the 1950s and 1960s.

Kenwood's third and final farewell hit the news on Thursday, March 23, 2023, when the entire building was brought to the ground by a catastrophic fire. No one was injured, as the building was still unoccupied. The shock of the fire brought forth memories from the nuns who had lived there so many decades ago. I myself was surprised at the emotional attachment I witnessed to a building that was really only a building now. We had moved out, along with all our things, and we sold the building long ago. The nearby cemetery, where generations of sisters rest, was untouched by the fire.

Religious life in the twentieth century experienced the boom and bust of a rapidly changing social landscape. Now in the twenty-first century, the bust continues, as we see the growing smallness of our communities. Sometimes religious life today feels like we are continuing to hold on to what no longer makes sense. Community life is not what it used to be: institutional living is not the norm anymore, though it still exists in many places. In fact, institutional living is making a comeback as sisters in their elder years move from small communities to places where their daily needs can be met more easily. Those of us who are not ready for that life change are left behind in houses that have aged badly, without repairs or updating, with empty rooms and the belongings of other people (oh, the books and CDs I have seen left behind!). The few "younger" sisters rattle around in space that no longer serves, living a religious life that doesn't meet our needs any longer either.

The picture is not really that dire, though changes are certainly needed. But we don't make changes without honoring what has come before and the gifts that we have received. Those sisters who received novitiate formation at Kenwood are the same ones who lived through the dramatic changes of the Second Vatican Council. They are the sisters who entered expecting silence and stability, only to find that they were then asked to form small communities (without training as to how), to reach out to the world beyond the cloister (which no longer existed), even to choose clothing that was no longer that of widows living one hundred fifty years earlier. While those changes were external, they marked incredible internal changes as well. Sisters who thought teaching would be their lifelong task began to imagine themselves in other ministries, perhaps even ministries that better suited their gifts.

Sisters began to study theology even more than before, and they learned from the theological fathers (yes, fathers) of Vatican II. Opening up to the world meant interacting with it differently. Just as the whole church was opening up, so too the sisters began to step out of their training into new situations. With the opening of the stained-glass windows came societal changes that opened new possibilities: women's rights, civil rights, disability rights came hard-fought, the language of "liberation" became more commonplace in all sorts of contexts, and sisters placed themselves wherever they felt God's most vulnerable called them. With these movements came the media revolution, such that news from across the globe became more and more present with less delay. Sisters in the US joined in the call for the government to stop participating in violence in other countries, whether through arming and training guerilla fighters or creating nuclear weapons. Missionary women and men lost their lives for their outspoken criticism of oppressive regimes.

While all of these explosive and society-changing revolutions were happening, most women religious kept living, their every action devoted to the mission they chose to serve, witnessing to the presence of God in our world in everyday ways. These ordinary religious were extraordinary, too—witnesses to the profound changes in the world and in religious life, they chose every day to remain faithful to the call and the vows that led them to the convent in the first place. Without every single one of these women, we would not be here today.

And yet, our epoch is one of change, too. We have seen the world change more rapidly than we could imagine. Studies have shown that the changes happening are exponentially increasing all the time.[7] Our own experiences tell us that the events of the last five years have irrevocably shifted our ways of thinking and being in this world. The profound division between one side and the other on every social, political, and ecclesial issue has ruptured society such that it's difficult to have a conversation with someone who disagrees. The media attention finally given to the racist structures in society has both fed that division and at the same time opened people's eyes to realities they could ignore previously. Incredible waves of migrants shed light on climate destruction and unacceptable levels of violence throughout the world, affecting those living in poverty

[7] See Aneel Chima and Ron Gutman, "What It Takes to Lead Through an Era of Exponential Change," Harvard Business Review, October 29, 2020, and William D. Sheridan, "Exponential change applies to everything—not just technology," Business Learning Institute, January 4, 2021.

more than any other group. A worldwide pandemic forced everyone—not just the most vulnerable—to see how much we depend on one another and just how vulnerable everyone is.

The second half of the twentieth century saw disruption that only started this exponentially growing ball rolling. How do we respond to the giant changes society is throwing at us, here and now?

This Collaborative Project

This book emerges from an awareness of the need for change, the demand that *we* change. Equally, this book emerges from the recognition that religious life is enduring, timeless, and has something fundamentally important to teach the world. The tension that exists there—between the needs of today and the timeless nature of our life—is exactly where we start our conversation.

We seek to provide fuel for contemplation and commitment to the reseeding side of the equation. While the authors fall into the category of the Next Generations,[8] usually referred to in religious life circles as "newer" or "younger" members, this conversation is by no means limited to the minority age cohort. The seeds of hope and possibility for the next chapter of religious life are alive among all the present generations. The time is now to tend religious life through the reseeding of abundance, charism, connection, diversity, inclusion, and sisterhood. These are the themes that the authors were invited to address, in whole or in part, from their own experience and perspective.

In the first chapter of this collection of essays, "Reseeding for Today and Tomorrow," Susan Rose Francois, CSJP,

[8] See chapter 1.

begins by reflecting on the profound change the dominant generation of today's sisters experienced following the Second Vatican Council. Just as our elder sisters entered religious life not knowing where it would take them, so too women religious today are on an adventure without a clear vision of the end result. Susan encourages us to take courageous risks into unknown territory, just like many of our founding persons did.

Tracey Horan, SP, shares the joy and vitality of the many intercongregational encounters that led her to her religious vocation in "Intercongregationality: A Contagious and Audacious Light." In this time of darkness, which holds both uncertainty and possibility, global sisterhood highlights the abundance religious life offers when creativity is allowed to reign. Sharing mission and dedication with one another broadens the tent of our religious life, allowing new growth where space is made for the seed to be sown.

Katty Huanuco, CCVI, starts with the question, "where is home?" Her answer is "where the future is," meaning where there is life, dreaming, joy, energy, and vulnerability. Finding herself in a new country, Katty celebrates the diversity of her community, which allows her to bring everything that she is to this new life. The global sisterhood helps complete us, reminding us that no individual has the fullness of life without others. We are called to nurture the global sisterhood, which brings us energy, greater knowledge, and fulfillment that we cannot find alone.

Within the context of the hierarchical church, the image of sisterhood guides Sarah Kohles, OSF, in navigating and even staying in the church when problematic or abusive behavior emerges. In "Sistering the Church: What Does It Mean for Women Religious to be in Right Relationship with the Catholic Church?" Sarah calls on her spiritual and religious ancestors, including Francis and Clare of Assisi, to help her stay in right relationship. Sarah playfully uses the image of being a sister to the church as a way to describe different roles we might take on.

In "Soul Sisters from Yonder," Chioma Ahanihu, SLW, gives witness of her experience as a woman who left her native land to live a religious vocation in the United States. In religious life today, these Global Migrant Sisters like Chioma bring many gifts to the community, including the ability to minister with people from different languages and cultures, adaptability, and the call to the dominant culture to make room for diversity. Chioma calls all of us to listen to the Spirit guiding us to what is ours to do in this time of great transition.

In her essay, "Reseeding in Scorched Ground: Reclaiming My Vocation to Religious Life," Ricca Dimalibot, CCVI, portrays her deeply personal struggle with the radical availability of working in medicine and in leadership of the community. She speaks of the moral injury of medical ministry through the COVID-19 crisis, and the cost of the language of diminishment, crisis, and unbelief. As a congregational leader, she articulates the paradox of her role to uphold an idealized vision for the world, paired with the struggle to maintain what is, and survive through crisis. In the midst of growing internal emptiness, Ricca sees Jesus working to draw her back to rest completely in his love.

Juliet Mousseau, RSCJ, in "We Need One Another," draws on the history of her congregation, both the sisters she has known and the foundational sisters, to recall the significance of charism. The charism of the congregation spoke to the needs of the time it was founded, and so it also speaks to the needs of today. Additionally, our respective charisms bring us closer to a global sisterhood. We need each other, she argues, because each one of us and our orders can only show a tiny sliver of the great plan of God for our world. The diversity of our different gifts contributes to the many needs of our world.

Expanding on the reseeding imagery found throughout this volume, Monica Marie Cardona, VDMF, in "Reseeding, Sprouting, and Rooting Deeply," writes of her experience in a newer form of religious life, one in which lay men and women, vowed religious, and priests share a charism, spirituality, mission, and governance. Though a younger order, the Verbum Dei Missionary Fraternity remains deeply rooted in the call of Christ and the original intent of the founder. These roots continue to hold them stable as the congregation and the world experience rapid changes and unpredictability. Images of plant life flow into the solid rock of contemplation, where we find strength to live out the Gospel.

Nkechi Iwuoha, PHJC, takes us out of ourselves into the wider context of our world in the essay "Reseeding Religious Life from the Lens of Integral Living." Our vows call us to live in harmony with others, especially those who are on the margins of society. Religious women are called to work in all areas of the world, cultural, economic, social, political, and spiritual, each one of which needs transformation to become more human, more holy, closer to the dream of God for the created world. The dream of religious life will continue to expand as we engage in prayerful and discerning listening, along with the whole church as it embraces synodality.

We invite the reader to consider this time in religious life not as one of crisis or despair but rather one of hope and possibility. Every generation of religious life experiences an urgent call to respond to the signs of the times. Now is our time. Let's reseed religious life for the present and the future.

1

Reseeding for Today and Tomorrow

Susan Rose Francois, CSJP

The "Next Generations" called to live religious life are a relatively small yet diverse cohort who answered the call to vowed life in the Global North in the late twentieth and early twenty-first centuries.[1] We are inheriting a large legacy from the generations that faithfully answered the call of the Second Vatican Council to read the signs of the times.[2] Blessed by their witness and companionship, we are strengthened and inspired to do what is ours to do, in our time, for the sake of the Gospel. We are further blessed with the ongoing love and support of our elder sisters, who continue to walk with us in faith and hope into this emerging

---

[1] I offer "Next Generations" as an alternative to the term "newer and younger members." An analysis of the 2023 Statistical Report from the National Religious Retirement Office shows that approximately 19 percent of women religious in the United States are under the age of 70. This represents a diverse group of four generations: younger Baby Boomers, Generation X, Millennials, and Gen Z.

[2] See "Inheriting Great Love and Responsibility" by Susan Rose Francois (*Global Sisters Report*, March 20, 2015) and "An Open Letter to the Great Generation" by Teresa Maya (*Global Sisters Report*, January 12, 2015).

future. What's more, we are energized and enlivened by a vibrant network of sister peers across congregations and continents, as evidenced by this book. Just imagine the possibilities.

Pope Francis has named our time not as "an era of change as much as a change of era."[3] From climate chaos to the decline and destabilization of social, political, financial, and religious institutions, the ground is shaky and the path forward uncertain. Amid all this noise and confusion, "God is still calling, and mature, accomplished, thoughtful, reflective women are still responding."[4] Rooted and nourished by our own institutes and charism families, we embrace the emerging understanding of the charism of religious life and the power of global sisterhood as signs of prophetic hope for fractured times. Following the Spirit's leading, we are called to risk the bigness of smallness as we reseed religious life with an abundance of hope, connection, and possibility in this change of era. The rest, thankfully, is up to God.

Change of Era

I often find myself reflecting on a conversation I had as a novice with Sister Mary Byrnes, CSJP, who passed away a few months later. Sister Mary graciously agreed to allow me to interview her about her experience before, during, and after Vatican II for an assignment for my history of religious life class. She shared that she'd entered in 1950 at

[3] Pope Francis, *Meeting with the Participants in the Fifth Convention of the Italian Church,* November 10, 2015. I was introduced to the concept of change of era by Mary Pellegrino, CSJ, in a presentation she gave to Peace Ministries and the Sisters of St. Joseph of Peace in February 2023.

[4] Michelle Lesher, SSJ, "Called to Revision Religious Life for the 21st Century" (presentation to the Sisters of St. Joseph of Peace Assembly, Spring 2023).

the age of twenty-one, thinking she'd be a teacher. Sister Mary did in fact spend many years in education. It was when she spoke of the period of renewal after Vatican II that she came most alive, sharing how her understanding of God and our community's charism of peace through justice expanded. She regaled me with stories of her travels as part of the Movement for a Better World and her friendships with people of other faiths.[5] I just sat there in her infirmary room and listened, enthralled, until she became suddenly quiet.

She confessed that she was in awe of those entering religious life today. She couldn't understand how we could even think of joining during this time of uncertainty and diminishment. I looked her in the eye and asked her if *she* had known, when she entered, that she would do all the things she had just told me about. "No," Sister Mary admitted sheepishly. "The only difference," I remember telling her, "is that you thought you knew what your religious life would be like. We come in now knowing that we have no idea."

Each generation is shaped by the ethos of their time. Like Sister Mary, Loretto Sister Mary Luke Tobin was part of a generation whose vocation was formed in the context of "a high sense of morale in the Roman Catholic Church, especially during the 1940s and 1950s." She reflected in her memoir: "Young women in large numbers (compared to the past) began to crowd novice ranks. Our Catholic enthusiasm, not to say triumphalism, during this period seemed justified by our expanding numbers."[6] Reflecting back from the perspective of history, I find myself smiling

[5] True to form, Sister Mary made sure that her Buddhist monk friends were invited to her wake, where they chanted prayers for their friend.

[6] Mary Luke Tobin, SL, *Hope Is an Open Door: Journeys in Faith* (Nashville: Abingdon, 1981), 48.

at the sneaky ways of the Holy Spirit, drawing these young women to fill the ranks of religious life on the cusp of major changes they could not imagine.[7] Their creative energy and enthusiastic leadership fueled the faithful response to the call for the adaptation and renewal of religious life in the decades that followed.[8]

I don't think you could honestly say that there is a high sense of morale in today's church. My archdiocese had just declared bankruptcy in the wake of the sexual abuse crisis when I began to discern my religious vocation in 2004. While I had grown up Catholic and attended twelve years of Catholic school, I had only returned to the active practice of my Catholic faith five years earlier, after a twelve-year "vacation" as a young adult, during which I alternated between agnostic and almost atheist. I smile at the name of the Nuns & Nones movement, given that I am a cradle Catholic turned none and now a nun. In the complex ethos of our time, there is a clear desire for spiritual connection and work for the common good, even as we are losing trust in and relationship with the institutions that formerly sought to meet that need. This is the context that birthed the vocational call of the Next Generations of religious.

My personal experience leads me to agree with Sister Michelle Lesher, SSJ, "that it is a miracle that any one of us responded to this call," let alone that "many communities . . . have had the desire and the capacity to continue to make space to welcome newer members."[9] Just as I told Sister Mary Byrnes all those years ago, the women entering

---

[7] Sister Beth Taylor, CSJP, my formation director and friend, often spoke of the "sneaky" Holy Spirit, able to find a way through any crevice or opening.

[8] Pope Paul VI, *Perfectae Caritatis (Decree on the Adaptation and Renewal of Religious Life)*, 1965.

[9] Lesher, "Called to Revision."

religious life during this change of era, when large-scale religious life is receding, know that our future will look and feel very different.

I find it significant that one learning from the listening sessions organized by Leadership Conference of Women Religious (LCWR) as part of their national discernment process on the emerging future of religious life—so revelatory it made it into an official document—is that the younger cohort are "FEARLESS about this."[10] Not only are the Next Generations generally unafraid, we have a shared sense of excitement about what might be possible in a less institutional and smaller-scale religious life, rooted in connection and collaboration across porous borders.[11] Moreover, I dare to believe that during this change of era, God is calling forth the exact number and diversity of women religious needed for our present and near future. It's all about perspective and how you choose to view and engage the chaos swirling all around us.

It is understandable that some observe "diminishing numbers, advancing age, few if any vocations, increased tensions between the demands of maintenance and the call to mission, a smaller pool of willing and able leaders, and actuarial tables that only project a continuation of these trends,"[12] and wonder if there even is a future for religious life, especially when current challenges are viewed from the

---

[10] Leadership Conference of Women Religious, "What We Are Seeing: An Analysis of Conversations about Religious Life as it Moves into the Future," February 2022, 6. Capital letters in original.

[11] An earlier LCWR dialogue process led to the development "The Emerging Orientations" in 2020. One orientation was to widen the tent with more porous borders across congregations, organizations, generations, and cultures.

[12] Ted Dunn, "Refounding Religious Life: A Choice for Transformational Change," *Human Development* 30, no. 3 (Fall 2009): 7.

perspective of the structures and narratives of the past. Many leadership teams and communities have already discerned between known structural choices, such as reconfiguring (merging with other units of the congregation) or coming to completion (making the decision to no longer accept newer members).[13] This work is necessary, important, and morally responsible. It is also primarily, though not exclusively, the work of the dominant age cohort, who entered large-scale religious life and navigated the winds of change following renewal.

I was first elected to congregation leadership in 2014. Even as a member of the Next Generations cohort, I too have been engaged in these receding tasks, both in my leadership for my own community and as a former member of the LCWR National Board. No matter where a community finds itself in its life cycle, responsibly tending to the receding of large-scale religious life must go beyond structural change and deep into the very heart of mission. Receding work can be daunting and exhausting, yet at its core, it has the potential to be life-giving. It is ultimately about creative love.

The Other Side of Chaos

In his keynote presentation at the 2023 LCWR Assembly, evolutionary cosmologist Brian Swimme placed this critical work in the widest context—cosmic spirituality. "The explosion of a star is a primary revelation of love at a cosmological level. . . . A love exemplified by the history of Catholic sisters. A love that reveals the heart of divinity.

---

[13] Faced with our demographic reality, my own congregation made the decision to suppress our three autonomous provinces and become one congregation without provinces in 2008. I have served on the second and third congregation leadership teams elected since that decision.

The star dies in its final act of generosity, and out of that generosity, the future of the universe is born."[14]

Sitting in the audience, surrounded mostly by elected and appointed religious life leaders of the dominant age cohort, I felt a sense of immense personal freedom. My heart interpreted what Brian Swimme said this way: large-scale religious life, like a supernova, is meant to explode, so as to give birth to smaller-scale religious life. What *was* must recede, so that new expressions and experiences of religious life can emerge, in creative love, for this time.

I sense a growing awareness in religious life circles regarding this call to engage in reseeding work, both in the Next Generations and among many of our elder sisters, even as large-scale religious life recedes during chaotic times. Sister Patricia Murray, IBVM, executive director of the International Union of Superiors General, observes that there have always been "periods of decline and growth" in religious life. "It has been precisely during these times of diminution that the seeds of the new have been sown, which have led to a new understanding of the meaning and purpose of religious life and the emergence of new forms or new emphases."[15] Awareness of the call to reseeding work during this change of era, however, is not the same as knowing *how* to engage, or even dare I say *embrace*, this work as the sacred task of our time.

The nature of this reseeding work becomes clearer when, in the words of author Margaret Silf, we view the change of era from the "other side of chaos." God's action "on the raw material of creation gives us a clue" for what is

[14] Brian Thomas Swimme, "Cosmological Spirituality of Catholic Sisters" (keynote presentation, LCWR Assembly 2023), 8.

[15] Patricia Murray, "Foreword," in *God's Call Is Everywhere: A Global Analysis of Contemporary Religious Vocations for Women* (Collegeville, MN: Liturgical Press, 2023), ix.

ours to do during our time. Silf reminds us that "a new energy can emerge, or even erupt" through the chaos of God's creation and "new possibilities can 'foam forth,' one by one, instant by instant."[16] The creative action of God may be large, but it can also be small. It can be obvious, or it can be hard to see. Chaos can be messy and anxiety producing. Chaos can also be exciting and filled with opportunities for the emergence of new movements, networks, and forms. I am increasingly convinced that the work of this time is to reseed the proverbial soil with nutrients—such as abundant hope, the power of connection, and creative possibilities— that will nourish, recognize, and support new life as it emerges among us.

Reseeding work is about creating hospitable spaces within religious life for what is emerging, rooted both in our particular and global charisms, to meet the wants of our age today and into tomorrow. Our task is not so much to manage or control the chaos, but rather to lean into the unknown with creativity and hope so that new life takes root, grows, and cross-pollinates in service of the Gospel through the intentional living of global sisterhood.

Reseeding is not meant to be a naïve or Pollyannaish framework—quite the contrary. We cannot ignore our realities, be it the violence on our streets, climate chaos, or religious life demographics. Taking a long, loving look at our religious reality and that of the wider world necessitates coming to grips with a great deal of loss and grief.[17] I have long wondered if my age cohort of women religious, we who have lost so many of our wisdom women friends early

---

[16] Margaret Silf, *The Other Side of Chaos: Breaking Through When Life Is Breaking Down* (Chicago: Loyola Press, 2011), 46.

[17] See Susan Francois, "A Loving Gaze at Religious Life Realities," *Horizon* (Fall 2013).

in our vocations, are being prepared for service as practitioners of love and loss, grief and hope in a church and world experiencing deep pain.

There is a growing sense of shared vulnerability among women religious of all ages, which I consider a good thing and, paradoxically, a source of strength during this change of era, with unexpected gifts and seeds for the future of religious life. For example, the relatively smaller numbers of peers in our home communities led leadership to encourage intercongregation formation programs and support participation in peer networks such as Giving Voice. Consequently, the Next Generations have always experienced an intercongregational dimension as core to religious life and central to our identity and sense of community as women religious. While I am blessed with a few age peers in my community—including some younger than myself—I have many more whom I call "sister" across congregations with whom I also share the charism of religious life. When I look to the future, one thing I know is that I will share the journey with these sister friends.

As governance responsibility and staffing of sponsored ministries shifts to dedicated lay partners, understandably a source of loss for some elder members who gave their life's work to those ministries and to our lay collaborators who mourn the presence of sisters walking the halls, the Next Generations are freed to live out the charism in less institutional ways. It simultaneously creates a wider and more diverse ministry family of support and connection. My understanding of my community's charism of peace through justice has only deepened and expanded as I see it lived out through the lives of our lay partners in mission.

Alliance and partnership are key principles for reseeding work. Gone are the days when we could—or should—be the ones running the show. Our elder generations of sisters

embraced the call of Vatican II to empower and support
the laity as key actors in the church and work for the common good. We know that what matters is the mission itself,
that it be mobilized, actualized, and shared for the good of
the whole. While I love religious life and believe in its future, this is also part of the reason why I have come to
believe that it makes sense if God is in fact *not* calling large
numbers of women to vowed religious life today. The want
of the age is not necessarily a large labor force of vowed
religious, or even a critical mass. This perspective shifts the
equation, once again, to the other side of chaos.

Reseeding work invites us to imagine ourselves as
"critical yeast," a concept I was introduced to through the
work of theologian John Paul Lederach. As critical yeast,
"a few strategically connected people have greater potential
for creating the social growth of an idea or process than
large numbers who think alike."[18] Note that important
word—a *few*. Is there a crisis of vocations if God is calling
us to be critical yeast for and with the church today, I wonder? Or could it be that the Spirit is calling the women we
need to be the critical yeast for today and tomorrow?

Lederach describes several characteristics of yeast which
are informative for discerning reseeding work. Yeast is
active and makes an impact through movement. It does not
work if it is static. Yeast needs a warm, hospitable environment to grow. To make an impact, yeast is kneaded and
mixed into the mass and has "capacity to generate growth"
beyond numbers.

The women who are answering the call today embody
this definition of critical yeast. Instead of engaging in meaningful ministry as single or married lay women, they are

[18] John Paul Lederach, *The Moral Imagination: The Art and Soul of
Building Peace* (New York: Oxford University Press, 2005), 91–93.

making the countercultural choice to live the vowed life in community. Applying Lederach's words, they are drawn to be "strategically connected" to a particular charism family and community, even as they engage in creative and collaborative work with others to build "capacity to generate growth" of the Gospel. The Next Generations of Catholic sisters may be few, but we are mighty. Connected across congregations and with networks of like-hearted people, we hope to live a life of love and service in community for the common good for decades to come.

It is crucial that religious communities who are open to accepting new vocations engage in the reseeding work of becoming welcoming communities and building the capacity to support today's young women, as they respond to the call to make meaning and be of service in our changing world. This holds major implications for initial formation programs which must be adaptive, collaborative, flexible, and responsive, while also staying rooted in the nonnegotiables of religious life.[19]

My own religious community's leadership has made formation one of our top priorities, along with the necessary receding work, such as property decisions and ministry legacy. In fact, I recently added the role of candidate director to the varied hats I wear, accompanying young women who are discerning their call with us. Another of our leadership team members serves as novice director. A third leadership team member is our initial formation liaison, collaborating with the formation director. A fourth leadership team member carries responsibility for ongoing formation.

---

[19] Michelle Lesher, SSJ, "Revisioning the Canonical Novitiate for the 21st Century" (doctoral dissertation, Fordham University, 2021). Lesher names the nonnegotiables as call, prayer, spirituality and discernment, community, apostolic mission/ministry, identity, and the vows, each considered through the lens of charism.

The wisdom of the renewal period would tell you that you should not mix leadership and formation ministry. There are indeed valid considerations when it comes to discernment and decision making which must be attended to appropriately and in consultation with canon lawyers. And yet, when I think back to the early years when the seeds of our charism were first planted and took root, our pioneering women wore multiple hats.[20] Perhaps as we read the signs of the times and lean into the bigness of smallness, we are invited to embrace that spirit once again and take some risks.

We also have the benefit of our lived experience, and so we have invited a wider group of sisters and associates of all ages to form a think tank to help reimagine formation and vocation ministry during this change of era, the youngest in her early forties and the eldest in her mid-nineties. The resulting creative energy, where the hope, possibility, and responsibility for vocation and formation work is held by many and not just a few, seems to be bearing some fruit in our community.

Ongoing formation is also critical to reseeding work, work which belongs to all the present generations living religious life. It is important to engage the entire community in prayerful discernment, contemplative dialogue, and meaningful action that nourishes dynamic growth of the present and future of religious life. This applies to communities that have made the decision to come to completion, as well as to those who are welcoming new members. Each sister has vowed to live the mission until her final breath. Our growing understanding of global sisterhood

[20] See below the example of Mother Evangelista Gaffney, who served as the first Superior General of the Sisters of St. Joseph of Peace as well as mistress of novices and postulants.

and the charism of religious life invites all generations to support the present and future of religious life in creative ways, by prayer and sharing of resources, for the good of the life itself.[21]

This reseeding time invites us to embrace a stance of holy curiosity and suspend the need to know how it all will work out in the end. This is equally true for all age cohorts, whether we hope to live this life for another thirty to sixty years or anticipate going home to God in the nearer future. What might this look like?

In her 2023 LCWR keynote address, theologian Jung Eun Sophia Park, SNJM—herself a member of the Next Generations cohort—offered the example of *Alice in Wonderland* to the assembled leaders as a model for this time in religious life. "Picture Alice, standing in front of the rabbit hole, through which lay an unknown mystery and an unknown future. Alice's curiosity draws her into the mysterious hole, and pulls her through it and onto a great journey. Like Alice, we religious are also invited on an adventure in this new world."[22]

Return to the Roots

If we are honest, in some ways this moment in religious life is not all that different from our founding stories. Our founding women and men also embraced holy curiosity and went on an adventure into the unknown to serve the Gospel. They had no idea what lay ahead, and yet here we

---

[21] For example, see the Designated Fund for the Emerging Future of Religious Life established by LCWR, accessed March 12, 2024, https://www.lcwr.org/resources/fund-emerging-future-religious-life.

[22] Jung Eun Sophia Park, "Three Journeys to the Mystery" (keynote presentation, LCWR Assembly 2023), 4.

are today, because of their faith, courage, and witness. Today's reseeding work must be rooted in our histories.[23]

It was only after I started working on this project on reseeding that I realized how much my own community's founding story is rooted in the imagery of seeds. At the profession of our very first sisters in Nottingham, England, in 1884, Bishop Edward Gilpin Bagshawe said to the new community: "You will hope, if God blesses your work, to sow the seeds of peace in modern society."[24] We borrowed this phrase for our 2008 Chapter Act, *Seeds of Peace*, calling us to grow in nonviolence and care for creation.[25]

Mother Evangelista (Honoria Gaffney) was one of the sisters who professed vows that day in St. Barnabas Cathedral. Just four years later, after the tumultuous departure of our founder, Mother Francis Clare (Margaret Anna Cusack), she became the first Superior General.[26] She experienced firsthand the challenging early years of the congregation, which she later described to another bishop as filled with "poverty, humiliations, trials, difficulties, disappointments, failures, etc."[27] Chaos, it seems, was familiar to Mother Evangelista. I believe she must have had a deep spiritual life to provide such steady leadership as she navigated the choppy waters of our early decades.

I find glimpses of the spiritual roots which surely nourished her in our congregation archives, including a

[23] See Teresa Maya, "Backwards to Move Forwards: History Matters in Formation," *InFormation* (Summer 2023).

[24] "The Sisters of Peace in the Diocese of Nottingham," *The Tablet* (January 12, 1884), 72.

[25] Sisters of St. Joseph of Peace, *Seeds of Peace: Acts of the 21st Congregation Chapter*, 2008.

[26] See Dorothy Vidulich, *Peace Pays a Price: A Study of Margaret Anna Cusack* (Englewood Cliffs, NJ: Kenmare Press, 2019).

[27] Mother Evangelista Gaffney, "Response to the Bishops' Questions," 1920.

collection of reminiscences from those who had Mother Evangelista as their formation director. One story shared by Sister Stanislaus is especially informative. Not only did Mother Evangelista encourage the young sisters to "aim at striking deep roots," she gave them a practical demonstration, taking them one day to the greenhouse where the gardener had sown seedlings. "There they nestled in the moist clay and in time produced deep roots. Later on good sturdy plants appeared—a good lesson and an inspiring one at the beginning of one's postulancy."[28]

We have another gem in the archives from Mother Evangelista, namely her last words, reportedly said to the sisters gathered around her in Nottingham as she lay on her deathbed: "Stick to your colours. Uphold the simplicity, unity, and family spirit that have always animated and been the distinctive character of our Community. . . . Be kind to one another."[29] In other words, stay rooted in who we are and nourish each other with your everyday actions. Her final words to the community have a particular relevance for her sisters today, as we seek to live into the call of our 2022 Congregation Chapter—*To Be Who We Say We Are.*[30]

I imagine Mother Evangelista must have reflected on the Parable of the Sower (Matt 13:18-23). She seemed to instinctively know that seeds sown on rocky ground—such as a community experiencing division or floundering in despair—would not and could not flourish. Rather, seed sown on rich soil, nourished by shared values, hope and

[28] Sisters of St. Joseph of Peace, *Revised Tribute to Mother Evangelista*, 1965.

[29] Sisters of St. Joseph of Peace, *Mother's Advice to Us from her Deathbed*, 1920.

[30] Sisters of St. Joseph of Peace, *To Be Who We Say We Are: Acts of the 23rd Congregation Chapter*, 2022.

love, "bears fruit and yields a hundred or sixty or thirtyfold" (Matt 13:23).

Seeds Sown for Today and Tomorrow

In this change of era, we are called to reseed religious life with an abundance of hope, through the connections of global sisterhood and with the power of possibility thinking, for today and tomorrow. While we do this in our present-day context, this is who we are and always have been as followers of Christ.

In the same 2015 address where Pope Francis reflected on our time as a change of era, he observed that the church is always called to reform itself. However, he cautioned that this constant call to renewal "does not end with the umpteenth plan to change the structures. Instead, it means to be grafted and rooted in Christ by letting oneself be led by the Spirit. Then everything will be possible with genius and creativity."[31] Everything is possible with God. Reseeding work prioritizes this perspective on the other side of chaos.

Just think about the reseeding work Pope Francis has invited the global church to engage in through the emphasis on synodality, returning to our own church's roots. While the Second Vatican Council opened wide the doors of the church and called for the renewal of religious life, today's church—and religious life—is again being invited to follow the Spirit's leading into the questions, without a roadmap, or even a particular agenda through the evolving synodal process.

Sister Mary Luke Tobin, one of only fifteen women invited to the Second Vatican Council as auditors, observed

---

[31] Pope Francis, *Meeting with the Participants in the Fifth Convention of the Italian Church.*

that a "door marked 'change' was quietly opening to a much wider vision of the church and of religious life."[32] Writing in her memoir two decades after the council, she remained hopeful: "I think we can say that, although so much remains to be done to implement the council's initiatives, the seeds sown are taking root and growing. We may be like the man in the Gospel story who, after sowing the seeds, went about his business, and one day was surprised at their growth."[33]

In no small part due to the influence of women like Mary Luke Tobin, religious life changed rather quickly in the years after Vatican II, while the wider church tends to change more slowly. Yet even the institutional church can surprise us with its own reseeding work. During the October 2023 session of the Synod on Synodality, for example, seventy non-bishop members were present, with half of these being women, including Sister Nathalie Becquart, XMCJ, undersecretary of the Secretariat of the Synod and one of the highest-ranking women in the Vatican. These women were present as voting members, not auditors like Mary Luke Tobin—a significant change, the impact of which will only become clear in time. Even if the results do not meet expectations, hopes, or desired timetables, this creative and courageous reseeding work is worth the risk.

Yes, reseeding can be risky business. "The seed must lie in the ground, and the new growth must break through the cold earth."[34] There are no guaranteed outcomes. "By definition, risk accepts vulnerability . . . [and] means stepping into a place where you are not sure what will come or what will happen."[35] It is good then that we are becoming more comfortable with vulnerability, both in the personal and

---

[32] Tobin, *Hope Is an Open Door*, 48.

[33] Tobin, 35.

[34] Silf, *Other Side of Chaos*, 139.

[35] Lederach, *Moral Imagination*, 163.

collective sense. Reseeding invites us to embrace our vulnerability as a superpower of sorts, a much-needed witness to the world.

Reseeding work calls us to expand our horizons, beyond the familiar boundaries of our communities or even continents. Sister Anne Munley, IHM, observes that there is a "shift in understanding of charism" as "a both/and awareness of the significance of particular charisms and the pull toward a broader sense of the charism of religious life as a whole . . . manifested in growing identification and appreciation for the collective potential and impact of the global sisterhood."[36]

Put simply, in reseeding times, religious life anywhere is religious life everywhere, and it is all good. "Wherever one of us ministers," we say in my community, "we are all present." We are coming to understand that this applies not only within our institutes, but across the global sisterhood. Imagine the possibilities that emerge with this growing understanding! Like Alice, we are called to go down the rabbit hole into the unknown. Global sisterhood means that we have companions and co-conspirators on this Gospel adventure, within our communities and across porous borders.

What might happen if we resisted the urge to plan, to figure out the way forward, and instead focused our energy on leaning into our vulnerability to create networks of mutuality, support, and creativity? I have seen glimmers of what can happen when we focus on this central reseeding task. So have you.

We need only look back to our founding sisters. They really had no idea what they were doing. They were in tune

---

[36] Anne Munley, IHM, "Learnings from the Collaborative Leadership Hubs" (presentation at the LCWR Assembly, 2022), 3.

with the Spirit, on fire for mission, and emboldened by the support of community. They took courageous risks together. They served the needs of their age and planted seeds for their and our tomorrows. We stand on their shoulders.[37] This is in our DNA. In the wise words of co-author and sister friend Sister Sarah Kohles, OSF: "We've got this."

---

[37] See Susan Francois, "Standing on the Shoulders of the Women Who Went before Us," *Global Sisters Report*, August 10, 2023.

2

Intercongregationality: A Contagious and Audacious Light

Tracey Horan, SP

Introduction

It was the Easter Vigil at our little parish in southern Arizona. This was our first Triduum at the parish since we opened a house of Sisters of Providence in the area, and my housemate and I were excited to find that they had prepared a bonfire outside to light the Easter candle. We huddled around as the stars shone in a way that echoed our excitement for this ritual. This is the night, the *Exsultet* would tell us. This is the night for liberation and rejoicing, for wickedness to be struck down and justice to become the rule of the day. This is the night.

As parishioners gathered around, the priest led us through the opening ritual and lit the Easter candle. I happened to be toward the front, perhaps drawn by my love of fire and anticipation of a moment in our Catholic rituals that embraces the unity of the spiritual and the physical. From where I stood toward the front, I began to notice a small group pressing in: people with candles they had brought from their homes (not the standard issue I was holding) lining up to get a chance to light their wicks directly from the Easter candle, which they seemed to believe was a better or brighter flame. I sat in judgment as I stepped back to allow them forward. I was disappointed that even this ritual that seemed so communal, a circle of us out in the open around a flame, could become hierarchical.

Within a few moments of stewing in my judgment, I looked across the arc at the people on the far side. I noticed that the flame from the Easter candle had passed quickly through our side of the circle, but a whole swath of people on the far side were standing in darkness watching the pushy cluster gather around the Easter candle. I realized at that moment that I had a choice: I could mope in my judgment, or I could walk across and share my flame. It would require stepping out of the circle, and perhaps drawing attention to myself. It would mean disturbing the seemingly understood order of things. Yet it felt right. I stepped out and walked over to the other side of the circle and offered my light. I probably only lit two candles, but the light spread quickly to others. There was something so beautiful for me about seeing how naturally the light of Christ shared itself, how in seconds the darkness on the far side became filled by little flames, both small and beautiful under a sky of stars.

This is the night. This is a time in which many of us cannot easily see the way ahead. Even so, there is light available to us. There is a choice available to us. We can live in a space of scarcity that clings to the grandiosity of the structures our elder sisters have known. Alternatively, we can take the small, fragile light we carry and allow the tradition that grounds us to urge us on into a risky, beautiful darkness full of possibility. We can be generous and bold with the tender, precious lights we carry.

The words and symbols of the Easter Vigil offer a beautiful metaphor for this moment in religious life. The darkness is both uncertainty and possibility. At the beginning of the Vigil, the darkness may seem to overwhelm the small lights. Yet those lights grow and multiply, as does the anticipation of those who have gathered to witness resurrection. We hear ancient tales of miracles, of creation and of liberation without which our current reality would not make sense. By the end of the Vigil, however, it becomes clear that we are not meant to simply enjoy these larger-than-life tales. We are meant to continue the story of resurrection with our very lives.

In a similar way, we newer arrivals to religious life relish gathering around the fire to hear of those who have gone before us and marvel at the courage of our founders who overcame persecution, poverty, disease, and grueling journeys to respond to the luring of the Spirit in their day. We come away from the fire—whether it be a campfire, a feast day celebration or the burial of one of our elders—with a renewed sense of our call to give life to this legacy today. This is the night.

Intercongregational Roots of a Vocation

Since before I entered formal discernment with the Sisters of Providence of Saint Mary-of-the-Woods, I had already experienced the generosity of a global sisterhood and had an awareness that sisters from various congregations had shaped the woman I was becoming.

Often when people ask me about the seeds of my vocation as a Catholic sister, I cite my time living with the Sisters of Charity of Cincinnati at Casa Caridad in Anthony, New Mexico. Those two years were significant to me for a number of reasons. I started my first real job after college, I had my first real experience of intentional community life, and I got to see religious life behind the scenes. I learned that some sisters drink beer, watch football, and even curse on occasion. They tell jokes and sometimes argue. I started seeing these women in all their humanity and all their faithfulness. I was inspired by their decision to move to the desert (what one sister described as "hell on earth") from greener places and live in a double-wide trailer because they wanted to be present to the people society had tossed aside and demonstrate with their lives that God had not forgotten them. I experienced the generosity of women religious in their fifties and sixties who opened their home to twenty-, thirty-, and forty-somethings searching for the whispers of their own vocation.

Although I had previously stayed with the sisters at Casa Caridad for a short time, and I do remember talking through some of the logistics in a meeting before I moved, I was surprised at how willingly they welcomed me into their home. I was a recent college graduate with no expressed intention of discerning religious life, although I did feel called to be part of this mission at the border in some way. We quickly began to form a community as three (and then four) associates and three sisters who desired to seek mercy and love justice together among the people of God.

I never would have survived my first year as a teacher without their support and patience with my harrowing tales of disrespectful eighth graders and tears at the end of difficult days. During those two years, sacred morning prayer, passionate dinner discussions, and downtime together framed a space of vocational discernment and wondering where my life was headed.

As I began to think more seriously about religious life, naturally I considered joining the Sisters of Charity. I had been inspired by these women who had opened their home to me and whose life choices and focus of energies for the common good resonated with who I want to be. I began a formal process of discernment with them even as I moved back to Indiana to volunteer at the Sisters of Providence eco-justice center in Saint Mary-of-the-Woods, Indiana.

As I lived at the Sisters of Providence motherhouse and got to know their charism and founding story, however, I felt torn between two loves. I sat with gratitude to the Sisters of Charity for opening my heart to this call and showing me what it means to live the Gospel with generosity every day even while I felt a growing pull toward the Providence charism.

In the midst of this turmoil, I returned to Casa Caridad for a visit and to watch my former students graduate from eighth grade. I carried serious discernment questions in my heart and expected that the sisters at Casa Caridad would answer them for me. I shared about my life on the farm, and waited for them to start convincing me to get on with it already and join the Sisters of Charity. They did no such thing.

Instead, after they had listened to me talk about the eco-justice center for a time, one of the sisters commented, "Tracey, when you talk about the Sisters of Providence, you get this light on your face." Another agreed and said that she noticed I did not have that same light when I talked about becoming a Sister of Charity. I was angry and shocked that these sisters seemed to be cheering for the wrong team, against their own interests.

It took me a few days of processing and inner listening to realize that they were right. My heart was being lured to the Providence charism, as much as I tried to fight it. It took even longer for me to realize what a generous act this had been. These women could have easily tried to steer me toward their congregation, and that is precisely what I expected them to do. Instead, they desired for me to be fully alive. They wanted the light they saw in me to grow, and they knew it would flourish on the path to which I was being called.

Such generosity can only flow from a global sisterhood that celebrates the gifts of each charism and can see the bigger picture. These women knew that my thriving would benefit the people of God and the common good, and that our sisterhood was not limited by the structures of our congregations.

This generosity and cross congregation collaboration is nothing new. In fact, I learned as I studied the origins of the Sisters of Providence that as our founding sisters traveled across the Eastern United States in 1840 by steamboat and stagecoach to found a mission in the forests of Indiana, they received hospitality all along the way from the Sisters of Charity. In that way, my own origin story echoes that of my foundresses. These women seem to be spurring us on still today to lean on one another as we look beyond congregational structures to a more porous, light-sharing global sisterhood.

Prayer and Ministry

A couple years into my first full-time mission after full-time formation at our motherhouse, I discerned to move to House of the Little Flower, the Catholic Worker community in Indianapolis. I had struggled living with sisters who were all at least thirty years my senior in a rich suburb on the north side of town even as my ministry had me visiting trailer homes and working-class neighborhoods in parts of the city where gun violence was rampant. I knew, though, that as the only religious sister in the House of the Little Flower, I would need to fill my cup with regular common prayer in some way. I reached out to a group of Franciscan sisters who lived a ten-minute drive away to see if they would be willing to allow me to join them for morning prayer. They agreed.

The first time we sat down to pray together and I opened the familiar *People's Companion to the Breviary*, an inclusive set of the Liturgy of the Hours compiled by the Indianapolis Carmelites, I felt such a comfort in our shared sisterhood. I closed my eyes and imagined all the times, and all the places, where I had prayed these psalms with other sisters. My heart swelled as I listened to the sisters' personal intentions, which included justice issues of the day as well as prayers for their own infirm sisters. It felt like home.

As we chatted afterward, I learned that these women knew my two great aunts, who I did not really remember, but knew had been Franciscans in their congregation. They shared that one of them had been missioned to Mexico for a time. They said my current ministry with Mexicans and other Latinos reminded them of her. The feeling of home deepened.

The following year, my discernment led me back to the southern border to a ministry that would connect my experience as an educator and community organizer with my desire to transform US immigration policy. The ministry seemed to match my experience and gifts perfectly, but there was one problem: I could not convince any sisters from my congregation to move to the border with me. I had initiated some conversations and sent invitations to about a dozen sisters I thought might be open to the possibility, but for one reason or another, each of them responded that they could not make such a move at that time.

I desired to live in community with other sisters and knew that I could not sustain such an intense ministry in a new place living on my own. I noticed as I looked over the organization's website that there were other sisters on staff from a Mexican congregation, the Missionaries of the

Eucharist (Misioneras de la Eucaristia). I reached out to the superior of the house, María Engracia Robles Robles, and we set up a video call. I showed up with sweaty palms and my list of questions about their charism, their prayer life and structure around meals and chores. I was surprised when they had very few questions for me. They looked at each other and back at me, and Sister Engracia said, "¡Bienvenida!" (Welcome!)

So began three years of intercongregational, intercultural living in Nogales, Sonora, México. I did not realize when I moved in that this was the first time the Missionaries of the Eucharist had ever opened one of their convents to a sister from another congregation (let alone another country). It was a major adjustment for all of us, and even so, the riches and learnings were many.

This expression of intercongregational solidarity was mutually beneficial in a number of ways. At a practical level, I found a supportive community in which to live, and the Missionaries had income from my rent and another sister in the rotation for cooking and leading prayer. At a deeper level, we each became more aware that what we shared in common—our vows, our commitment to live the Gospel in community with others—outweighed the differences of language and prayer style and charism.

Our life together challenged the American-centrism all too prevalent at the border. I will never forget the first time I cooked for the house. Sister Engracia commented to me, "It feels strange to have a US American cooking for us and serving us. It's usually we Mexicans who do that for Americans." As a US American, I had chosen to live in Mexico, which was hard for some people to understand, especially in a context where many people risked their lives to cross to the United States.

Our mixed community also called our own prejudices into question. A few months into my time living in Nogales,

I acknowledged to the Missionaries that I had assumed they would be much more traditional and that I would have a hard time adapting to their spirituality and prayer style. I had been surprised to find songs and poems and prayers focused on justice and radical Gospel living. The missionaries admitted that they were surprised by my simplicity and assumed that a sister from the United States would be more materialistic.

During our time living together, we also welcomed a non-Catholic lay volunteer, who stayed with us for six months, and a Franciscan sister who joined us for a year. It seemed as though once the Missionaries saw that opening up their home to a sister from another congregation did not undermine their charism or their way of life, they began to open their arms wider and wider. As we reflected on those three years, we all acknowledged the challenges of navigating differences, but agreed that the richness of sharing our global sisterhood far outweighed the sacrifices we made.

In 2021, I was finally able, in some small way, to extend the welcome I had received from the Sisters of Charity and the Missionaries of the Eucharist to other sisters who felt called to come learn and minister at the border for a time. I dreamed up a program that would invite sisters to come and minister, but also to learn about policy dynamics and advocacy strategies for being part of the systemic change needed for migration with dignity. With the support of the executive director at my ministry, Catholic Sisters Walking with Migrants (CSWM) was born. Although I did not share a home with these women during their month-long stays, I accompanied them in the preparations, offered weekly reflections for them to process the experience, and trained them in advocacy tools and effective ways to transform conversations about migration. Each time I sat with one of the CSWM cohorts in prayer, I was filled with a profound sense of gratitude for our shared silence and God's presence among us. In this place of pain and possibility, hundreds of miles from our mother-house, whatever loneliness I might feel dissipated as I was renewed by their desire to join the work toward migration with dignity.

This shared ministry multiplied as sisters returned to their homes and offered presentations, spoke with local elected officials and United Nations representatives, and even considered how their congregational discernment might be shaped by the needs of people in migration today. Were they called to set up a new mission or host a family seeking asylum? How else could they respond? Each cohort, in reflecting on their time in Nogales, named the richness of connections across congregations and cultures and expressed a desire for these connections to continue and grow.

In 2022, a month after I professed vows, two Sisters of Providence joined me to set up Casa Teodora on the US side of the border so that I could continue my ministry with more support from my own congregation. The three of us committed to be a presence in this place, to live and participate, each in her own way, in the mission of migration with dignity at the border. A year later, a Franciscan Sister of Perpetual Adoration who had participated in the CSWM program discerned to join the house, and I was able for the first time to welcome someone from a different congregation into a house my sisters and I had founded.

Fanning the Flame

A decade after I began my formal process of discernment and formation as a religious sister, I know that I would not be the Sister of Providence that I am today without the Sisters of Charity, the Missionaries of the Eucharist, my Franciscan ancestors, and women religious from a dozen other congregations who have fanned the tender flame of Gospel life in me over the years. Together we have stepped out of the circles of congregational and institutional structure to offer our light to one another and to the world.

As I look around, I am buoyed by the knowledge that my story echoes in the intercongregational connections I see around me as women religious live into our global charism with generosity and hope. I see a congregation with resources funding another congregation's ministry. I see one of my own Sisters of Providence reach out to congregations she has never met to request hospitality as she treks across the country to bring one of our sisters to the motherhouse. I see how this outreach fosters connection and sisterhood beyond just a place to sleep. I see how intercongregational formation programs lead to lifelong friendships.

In these connections, I see an arc of women offering the flame of their vocations, their desire for shared Gospel living sustained by commitments to poverty, chastity and obedience. They cannot help but share their audacious light, a light that the world longs for and awaits. As they share this light, it grows and dances. Their foundresses and all the sisters who have gone before them rejoice and dance with them.

3

Home Is Where the Future Is

Katty Huanuco, CCVI

Coming back from my trip to San Antonio, Texas, for my sisters' jubilee, the cab driver who picked me up from the airport in St. Louis greeted me and, after few minutes on the road, she asked me: "Where is home? I mean, is this city home?" Immediately, I answered: "Yes. This is home!" To which she replied, "Welcome home." I smiled and told her, with words and with my facial expression, "Thank you." She and I talked about job challenges, especially for women of color like us, the diversity of cuisine in the city, and ended by encouraging each other to go to the African art festival. As I watched her leave, her question came back to my mind and heart: "Where is home?"

Where is home for a young consecrated woman today? As my experience is enriched and limited by time, space, formation, socio-economic status, and culture, these lines are only *a snapshot* or one *reel* of what I mean by home nowadays. It is my hope that some of this diversity, trust, joy, resilience, vulnerability, compassion, dreams, courage, authenticity, and faith will speak to you too about our gift and task of nurturing a global sisterhood today.

Home Is Where Life Is

Life may be simply the day to day and the choices one makes for today and tomorrow. As a Sister of Charity of the Incarnate Word, I live in a religious community which is multicultural and intergenerational. Actively learning and appreciating how to better welcome and celebrate the diversity among us and in our neighborhoods has been a Ruah's gift since our founding. In 1869, three young women, newly arrived from France, became one body to learn together how to heal, educate, accompany, advocate, support, journey, and get closer to God enfleshed in the concrete needs of the people and the territory of San Antonio, Texas. Invasion and war for the San Antonio lands led women, children, and the earth to cry out to God for healing and a dignified life. Fortunately, many women were committed to join forces so that this healing could occur. Home for them was tangible in time, location, and context. Home was characterized by diversity, trust, resilience, vulnerability, dreams, joy, hope, courage, and connection. That seed took root, spread, and expanded in many different ways.

Currently, my Incarnate Word community has vowed religious members from Peru, Ireland, the Philippines, Mexico, and the United States. We, as a congregation, also have a presence in Chile and Colombia through associates and collaborators from our ministries and partnerships. Witnessing this growth and change over my sixteen years of consecrated life has been a blessing. There are so many people, initiatives, and institutions nurturing a good life, the flourishing of life. There is so much love in the world. Indeed, I feel so proud of my younger and older sisters when they talk, pray, debate, and respond in the face of inequality, climate crisis, racism, violence, sexism, and exclusion. I have witnessed their radical love. Their courage, deep gladness, creativity, and caring make me believe and not be afraid. To listen to the stories and day-to-day experiences of my sisters is an opportunity to be inspired, emboldened, and challenged to continue sowing liberating seeds of life.

Love, justice, and freedom have not yet become a habit for many of us, our people, in our villages, in our societies, and in our world. There are many people and territories that are waiting for the relief from our hands. They are waiting for us. There is much good that we lack. It is urgent that we keep moving to encounter these individuals, cultures, and places. We need them in our lives so that we can live. Liberating ourselves to live the present and the future together with the people and their territories does us so much good.

Home Is Where the Present Is

I belong to this territory. Belonging for me is about the sort of power to co-create the structures that shape community. As a member of a religious community, I was invited to be here. I said yes. I remember that experience as a call from God to expand my heart. I was very happy in my beloved Lima when that call came to me. Those days, I sensed that I was doing something important for my religious community because I served as a liaison to the General Leadership Team (GLT) and my sisters. I was serving my local parish as an advisor to eleven youth groups. I was actively collaborating with different groups to promote justice, peace and care for creation. I was also leading the efforts of religious life in Peru to promote human rights. I definitely felt fulfilled at all levels (personal, communal, and ministerial). However, of course, I had challenges. It is not easy to push social change. I also felt the need to find time to acquire more knowledge that might help me to better serve those who are most vulnerable, those impacted by poverty.

When the GLT invited me to move from the mission in Peru to the mission in the United States, I listened. I remembered that in some international meetings I expressed the need to facilitate encounter and exchange opportunities that reflect more what we are and what we want to be. In fact, I heard something like what I had dreamed of: an international-intergenerational community. At that, I quickly said yes. Later, of course, I began to think about all that would be involved in leaving Peru. Several ghosts camouflaged as fears were inside me before I came to love St. Louis. One of my biggest fears was that I would not be able to communicate who I am. I did not speak English. The language barrier was one of the first and most real challenges I faced. Fortunately, my sisters in the community were on the same page. We all accepted to be in learning mode, willing to learn one another's language. Of course, this did not necessarily mean that all of them attended Spanish classes.

My first year in St. Louis was fascinating because, as members of the community, we represented our congregation's presence in the United States, Mexico, and Peru. In addition, the house was named the novitiate. Simply put, I felt that I was being invited to build community—a community called to be an intentional space that welcomes women in discernment. The community was meant to be just as we are: an international-intergenerational congregation. My present experience is my chance to make one of my dreams come true every single day. To do this, I needed to widen my heart even more, to be vulnerable, and to be born again. Everything around me was unknown, from the simplest things, such as mealtimes or what is considered spicy, to the more complex, such as the cultural-familial preference of how to address conflict. I started getting to know my sisters and learning English. Everything spoke to me of a new beginning—so challenging, so full of possibilities, and so full of energy.

Currently I am in the second year of my doctoral program in public and social policy, and I have immense gratitude to Ruth and Naomi's God. I also find myself surrounded by wonderful people in this new city of mine. For instance, my classmates and professors come from almost every continent on this planet. Furthermore, I have witnessed, during these four years in this community, the faith and passion for consecrated life of at least three young women with Mexican and Filipina roots. It is beautiful to contemplate them and their yes to their vocational call alongside us. I feel very blessed.

Unlike the millions of people who migrate by land, air, and sea, I was expected upon arrival, although I did not know the place or the people I would meet. I had a safe place to live. A community welcomed me to the city and the country. Like all people who migrate, to paraphrase Sr. Thea Bowman, *I come to this territory fully functioning. I bring myself; my Latina self, all that I am, all that I have, all that I hope to become. I bring my whole history, my traditions, my experience, my Peruvian culture, my songs, dances, languages, spirituality, teaching, preaching, healing and responsibility—as gifts to this territory.*[1] This is my present: who I am at home.

My few experiences in this country have made me feel different emotions about what it means to be a sister, a consecrated Latina today, here and now. It has certainly made my heart grow wider. To be fully a young consecrated

---

[1] Adapted from Thea Bowman, FSPA, "Address to the U.S. Bishop's Conference," June 1989.

Latina (and not in initial formation) in this church and society is not an easy task; but it is not the end of the world either, sister! Writing these lines, I smile. I am alive and happy. My heart is warmed by so much love that I receive every day. Life wins. It is true that, at times, I have wondered if other non-Latina, non-Black, or non-Asian sisters have experienced being treated as the last option or felt simply excluded, rejected. Preaching, reading, or leading an event or organization to predominantly white audiences can be complex and complicated. I wonder if, every time the police approach one of these sisters, they experience great fear rather than a sense of relief. Yes, I have seen how we treat people differently. I wonder if you have felt that, far from introducing you for who you are, people tend to talk about what you are doing in the country. Yes, I have experienced discrimination. I have felt excluded, unseen, marginalized, left out, and voiceless, a token person and a second-class member. Please don't misunderstand me and don't try to minimize my experiences or the experiences of many people in this country. No, it is not an exaggeration. It is real and painful. I also have felt loved, supported, accompanied, welcomed, acknowledged, and a sister with a voice and a vote. How could I not also remember those expressions and words of so many of my sisters who rejoiced with me, practically feasting for something that one does well.

These four years living in St. Louis have allowed me to have different experiences of community. That is the gift. And, naturally, I have sought professional help to heal. My heart is grateful for my spiritual director and also for my counselor. Yes, that is another of the graces in religious life: the courage and humility to seek help. These two people in addition to my closest friends are the ones who hold me tightly. My sisters in the congregation, my sisters in vocation, my sisters in the faith of the living God, the women of my salvation history, and my ancestors, all of them sustain my life. They are all my family. Yes, my family. In family, one can be totally honest, genuine, respected, and loved just as one is. Where one is free to be who one is, I call that space home.

Home Is Community

Now, everyone may have a myriad of ways to describe what community is. For me, community is a task and gift. When I reread my own stories and the history of my religious community, I realized that trust in the other, the others, the otherness, and the Other becomes primordial. The task of community requires trust. So, what does it mean to trust for a young consecrated woman living in an unfamiliar country that is not the one where she was born or raised in? Trust is trust, sister! I am positive that you know what I mean by that. Each person has a light that does good to us, to humanity. In that good we must trust.

As I speak about home as community, I reflect on my experiences in community life, the local congregational community, the parish faith community, the neighborhood community, and the larger community in the country. I have had the joy of living in different cities around my country and in Mexico. I have lived in communities with seven, six, five, four, three, and two members. Mostly, I shared my life and mission with my congregational sisters who were from different generations and cultures. So, for me, diverse community is home. In fact, I believe that we are living in an interconnected world, and every culture has a significant role in our common home.

My first intercultural experience was certainly Lima, the city where I grew up. Lima is known as *the city of all bloods. All Bloods* (*Todas las sangres*) is the title of the novel by Peruvian writer José María Arguedas that portrays the racial, regional, and cultural variety of Peruvian society. Lima is enriched with the greatest diversity of cultures, official languages, and mother tongues in all of Peru. To illustrate, I grew up speaking Spanish and hearing Quechua, the language of my parents. Having an accent means you know more than one language. That is, an accent is a source of pride. But in this country, the United States, for some people, an accent is something you should banish. Indeed, it seems that not having an accent may lead to fitting in.

Fortunately, I am Peruvian, a Latina. Far from looking to fit in, Peruvians tend to recreate. We nourish life by creating new ways. To illustrate, take a look at the number of different dishes Peruvians create with potatoes. All that we are we have learned from and with others. We need people. People do us good. Asking for help does a lot of good. Although it may seem countercultural in societies that tend to value self-sufficiency, I believe that asking for help is more akin to Gospel values. The tendency to be individualistic or to seek uniformity causes tangible damage. We need people to heal and remain open to encounter. We need to step out of the familiar to be okay with discomfort.

Although building a community does not depend only on oneself, one does nourish it. Community life needs to be recreated in order to fertilize the life of its members. Community life, for me, is sharing life with my sisters. Among sisters, the most important aspect is loving and caring for each other. Reciprocity is in place. Reciprocity means to acknowledge community members' assets and involve individuals as active persons in contributing to the community. So, the people who live with me are not my housemates, but my sisters. I am your sister even if I do not share your nationality, culture, or blood. Although the word *sister* does not automatically generate a healthy relationship in community life, it might be very good for us to remember it. As a good sister shared with me some years ago, a religious community is not a home where your chosen friends live, but rather your sisters chosen by God for you. As sisters, we seek every day to nurture a relationship of reciprocity and interdependence. Each sister is unique and was called like us to be a disciple, a Gospel woman.

Some of the cornerstones of both my consecrated life and my discipleship in this land have to do with the sorority that I experience, especially from my sister-mentor, my best sister-friends, and the sisterhood of the young consecrated-life community here in the United States that goes by the name of Giving Voice. When I talk to these women everything, everything makes sense. None of us tends to believe that we have it all figured out in life, and that is so good for us. They make me realize that I am neither the first nor the only one to experience such mixed feelings. They help me to look beyond. They walk with me. They cheer me on. It is the community of sisters where dreams are interwoven; they are shared. It is the space where one remembers and feels that one belongs to something much bigger. In this space, these young religious women are not only dreaming but also taking action. They have opened the windows and doors of their convent to be a home for women and children experiencing homelessness. They have dared to go and live on the peripheries of their cities or borders to welcome people who have been displaced from their countries and are looking for a dignified life. They say yes to graduate studies to ensure women's participation at all levels. They are in our streets, parishes, convents, and institutions mobilizing citizen participation so that democracy in this country is not only a valuable idea, but a daily reality for all. They work and collaborate in positions of leadership and accompaniment to make inclusion a reality today. Yes, these women are different in age, charism, spirituality, nationality, language, and profession. And yes, they are nurturing together a global sisterhood by creating spaces and bridges of encounter and relationships beyond the known.

All of my community experiences, both in this country and elsewhere, nurture the person I am today. I am alive! This life has been filled with joy, sadness, pain, anger, courage, and hope. I am aware that unlike so many poverty-impacted people, I have the privilege of choice. As we know from the news we read every day, not everyone in our neighborhoods has a choice. For me, fighting against this forgetting is a powerful way to do justice. Hope is something that I carry not only for me, but for the generations who will come. I ask the God of life to give me the courage to choose where I am most needed. I pray to feed my curiosity, even in frustration, so that I may grow. The multiple gifts of loving in community are worth it. They keep me open to love beyond measure. Blessed be God for all people who accompany our lives in a multitude of ways; they keep my heart warm.

Future Starts at Home

This place and its social, political, economic, and religious reality invite me to bear witness that this moment is a reseeding time. Our charisms are called to nurture a global sisterhood. It is impossible to live thinking only of oneself and the territory one is familiar with. We need others. We especially need people with diverse experiences and backgrounds. We need to be deliberately intentional to nurture exchange, collaboration, and unity in relationships of equality. A global sisterhood gives us the opportunity to widen our hearts even further. It makes us, as local and global sisters, not only collaborate equitably and justly, but also identify and reduce the inequalities that impede progress toward God's dream. I see this sign of sisterhood especially in all those opportunities for intercongregational collaboration, all those searches and responses to intentional bonding that you and I have already seen, heard and celebrated.

There is already global sisterhood among us. I see that sign of sisterhood in the growing number of women and men religious coming to the United States from Latin America, the Caribbean, Asia, and Africa. All those women and men who are already here accompanying our people in this territory. There are also all those in consecrated life who dedicated their faith and energy in other countries and are back among us. All of them are a gift of the Spirit among us. I wonder if we ensure enough room for them to tell us their stories. Listening to those experiences and their learnings might exponentially broaden our perspectives. Such relationships could be vital to the global sorority movement moving forward.

I am convinced that the day we rescue our purpose and dreams—even if people say this is hard or difficult to bear—we will see the path that will bring us closer to the will of the God of Jesus. Although the task may be far from simple, we are accompanied by a sisterhood that can already be felt at home. Let us identify, name, and embrace our fears. As I have experienced in the Gospel and in popular wisdom, the opposite of fear is love. Perhaps that is why so many women and men continue to stand and look forward: because of love, that love that makes us learn and unlearn. Let's trust that we are ready. I dream that more sisters will create opportunities to encounter and journey together to better accompany our people, those people and families who are already all over the world. Imagine sharing dreams, hopes, and life with so many others like you who love this common home. I see in this place, my home today, plenty of opportunities for global sisterhood. Let's gather dreams, strengths, struggles, joys, concerns, hopes. Let us dream again. There is a lot of knowledge built up in the experience of so many of our sisters, and there is a lot of energy stored in so many of us, your sisters. Maybe what is coming is not the default option or expectation, but something much, much better. So, as so many folks say around here when you visit them, *make yourself at home.*

4

Sistering the Church: What Does It Mean for Women Religious to Be in Right Relationship with the Catholic Church?

Sarah Kohles, OSF

Who do you turn to for support when you have no idea what to do? Who prays with you and for you when you are facing challenges? Who do you trust to be there for you no matter what? I am aware that I rely on my entire community of Franciscan saints, living and deceased, to help me discern my path forward in the mundane and difficult circumstances of life. For example, whenever I need to schedule a flight in the winter in the Midwest, I call on Sister Jordan Dahm to help me choose the best dates for travel. Jordan is my patron saint of weather. She has ensured my safe travel and helped me dodge winter storms for over a decade! I call on Sister Mary Elsbernd whenever I am working on a writing project. She is my patron saint of scholarship, as she taught me the ins and outs of research. When I'm pondering how best to respond to a situation with a student at Briar

Cliff University, where I teach theology, I call on the 193 Franciscan sisters who have walked the halls of the school before me. I count on their love of the students and continued care for the university to help nudge me toward a productive way forward. I rely on my communion of Franciscan saints, living and deceased, to pray for me, to guide me with their wisdom, and to inspire me with their lives of dedication to the needs of God's people.

My most soul-rending struggles have been in relation to the hierarchical structure of the Catholic Church. I have turned to my founders, Francis and Clare of Assisi, and Mother Xavier Termehr, when I'm in greatest need. They help me discern what it means for me to be in right relationship with the Catholic hierarchy. Over the years, my difficult encounters with clergy in ministry and religious life have included:

- Pointing out a priest's practice of favoring wealthier Catholic-school families while over-enforcing "the rules" (expectations for sacramental preparation) for public-school families. He responded that it was up to him and that "it's a pastoral decision."

- Watching brother priests more comfortable with ignoring what was unjustly happening than standing up for a sister in their employ. (I was only a witness and not personally involved, yet it greatly impacted me as a young, idealistic sister in initial formation.)

- Struggling with how to support a parish community that was reeling after a seminarian was charged with two counts of indecency with a minor.

- Reporting a priest (my boss) for abusive behavior.

- Negotiating my shock and anger about the Apostolic Visitation of women religious in the United States and the Congregation of the Doctrine of the Faith's doctrinal investigation of the Leadership Conference of Women Religious.

• Signing a mandatum (that was excessively coercive in its wording) in order to teach theology at a Catholic university.

As is evident in my experiences alone, being a woman religious (or even a human being!) in the Catholic Church can be challenging to negotiate. A part of me is so very done with patriarchal nonsense and abuses of power. Another part of me knows that I may never be done dealing with hierarchical nonsense. Scripture scholar Phyllis Trible notes that a careful reading of the story of the Fall demonstrates that patriarchy only existed as a result of sin (Gen 3:16).[1] Therefore, patriarchy—that is, one gender "lording over" another—is a sin. So, why have we enshrined the sin of patriarchy in "tradition?" Why do we continually perpetuate the harm done to others through misuse of power? As I wrestle with these questions, I keep coming back to the question: What does it mean to be in right relationship with the hierarchical structure of the Catholic Church?

Although I have not provided the details, every one of my above examples of struggling with the hierarchical structure of the church involved men misusing power over women. Leaning on the wisdom of the Franciscan saints helps me grapple with this reality. This same wisdom, I believe, suggests a way forward for women religious in the church in this moment in time.

[1] Phyllis Trible, "Depatriarchalizing in Biblical Interpretation," *Journal of the American Academy of Religion* 41, no. 1 (March 1973): 41.

Turning to Francis of Assisi

Francis of Assisi is well known for his insight that all of creation is his sister or brother. The sun and moon, the earth, wolves and worms, birds and crickets, and every human person was a sibling to Francis. Even "enemies" deserve to be treated as family.

Our brother clergy are certainly not enemies, even if there are some we struggle with.

Francis insisted on great respect for clergy, because it is through their ministry that we receive the sacrament of the Eucharist.[2] He similarly insisted that churches be kept clean and that all scraps of paper with any letters written on them be treated with reverence because those letters, if rearranged, could spell the name of God. Francis had a profound understanding of what it meant to be in relationship. Shortcomings and sin do not change the reality that we all belong to God and are sisters, brothers, and siblings to one another.

Francis's witness to remaining in relationship is challenging to imitate, especially when we have encountered many difficult relationships with our clerical brothers. When I was at a Giving Voice conference (a gathering of about seventy-five younger women religious) a few years ago, we were asked to stand in response to a number of questions as a way of quickly coming to know each other: Who is in formation? Who has made their final vows? Who is teaching in a Catholic school? Who is involved in retreat ministry? Who works in a parish? Out of all those younger sisters, not a single sister worked in a parish. That was

---

[2] Francis of Assisi, "Later Admonition and Exhortation to the Brothers and Sisters of Penance," 34, in *Francis of Assisi: Early Documents: The Saint*, ed. Regis J. Armstrong, J. A. Wayne Hellmann, and William J. Short (Hyde Park, NY: New City Press, 2001), 47–48.

startling to me—and also not surprising at all. Many sisters are no longer working in ministries that put us in direct contact with clergy. It is hard to work with a difficult relationship and potential abuses of power every day. It's exhausting to try to remain in a healthy relationship with patriarchal systems. So, many of us choose ministries where we can more readily see the fruits of our efforts.

When we face challenges with hierarchical structures, women religious may toss around the idea of becoming noncanonical, as though that were a serious option. (To me it feels like Texan politicians flirting with the idea of seceding from the union. They think it's cute, but no one really believes it will happen.) I don't think this is an authentic option for Franciscans, when Francis was known for promoting respect for the clergy, whose hands give us the Eucharist. Francis remained in relationship.

But when I hear that people have stopped going to church, I understand. Some parishes, presiders, and liturgies are not generally a source of nourishment for me. Some experiences of church merely make me angry rather than invite prayer. And yet the question haunts me: What does it mean to be in right relationship with the hierarchical structure of the church? I hear the whispers of Francis in the background: *What does it mean to be sister to all?*

I remain convinced that we transform the church by remaining in it. By insisting that something else is possible, by refusing to leave, and by taking up space and creating space for others, we transform the church from the inside.

In some sense, my relationship with the church is like my relationship with my family. I may strongly disagree with them on politics, but they are still my family, and I love them dearly. I cannot walk away from my family. This experience of remaining in relationship with family is also a model for me of remaining in relationship with the hierarchical aspects of the church.

- What does it mean to remain in relationship with the hierarchy?

- How does my attitude toward clergy change when I think of them as my brothers?

- How well are women religious negotiating this relationship?

Relying on Clare's Persistent Vision

While Francis offers a meaningful insight into remaining in relationship with the church through his naming of all creation as sister and brother, I cannot help but wonder if Francis had an easier time in his relationship with the clergy because he was male. When I've struggled the most, I've turned to Clare, and found her to be a greater source of inspiration.

Clare of Assisi is also a model of relationship. She washed the feet of her sisters, and chose the least desirable tasks within her monastery.[3] However, Clare lived her entire adult life fighting with the church she loved to live what she knew she was called to—the privilege of poverty. The church hierarchy of her day had no ability to imagine a religious life for women that did not involve owning property and remaining in enclosure. Yet, Clare felt called to live like Jesus, who had "nowhere to lay his head" (Matt 8:20). When Agnes of Prague, a woman Clare had never met, wanted to pattern her communal life after Clare's insistence on poverty, Clare wrote to her: "What you hold, may you always hold. What you do, may you always do and

---

[3] "The Legend of Saint Clare," in *Clare of Assisi: The Lady: Early Documents*, ed. Regis J. Armstrong (Hyde Park, NY: New City Press, 2006), 292.

never abandon."[4] Clare encouraged Agnes to remain strong against the hierarchical structures of the church that insisted on limited roles for women. Clare advocated for a form of life for women that the male hierarchy could not fathom. She created an innovative option by living religious life in a new way, and she supported Agnes in doing the same. By remaining faithful to her call despite what the popes of her day imagined for her, Clare created something that didn't exist before her in the church—a rule of life written by a woman. She received approval on her deathbed. No other woman had written a rule recognized by the church.

Clare reminds me to persevere when I'm struggling with the clergy. As wonderful and inspiring as Francis is, he did not have to deal with the additional burden of being a woman in the church—too easily ignored, silenced, sidelined, contained. Clare reminds me to persevere when I'm teaching queer theory in one of my theology lessons in order to include students who are otherwise shoved to the margins. Clare reminds me to be tenacious, to find a way to work with the impossible pastor or bishop to get things done for the sake of the people we serve. Clare invites women in the church to insist on following their call, no matter how limited the vision of our brother clergy. A wider, broader, inclusive vision helps to claim possibilities and stand in the truth of our call. Clare continues to encourage us with the same message she wrote to Agnes: "What you hold, may you always hold. What you do, may you always do and never abandon."

- What is your experience as a woman in the church?

- How are women called to change the church today?

[4] Clare of Assisi, "The Second Letter to Agnes of Prague," in *Clare of Assisi: The Lady*, ed. Armstrong, 48.

- What is Clare inviting us to always hold, always do, and never abandon?

Depending on Mother Xavier's Courage

I also find it useful to turn to the foundress of my own Franciscan community—Mother Xavier Termehr. When Mother Xavier and her young community came to the US and found themselves in Iowa City, they were poor and nearly starving at times. The priest who was "helping" them racked up debt on their behalf. The priest also tried to undermine Mother Xavier's authority as the foundress of the community by demanding an election of a new mother superior. However, her sisters were not having it, and they unanimously reelected her. The injustices and utter waste of women's energy caused by meddling men angers me. Mother Xavier had to leave the good people she served in Iowa City and sever the relationship with that priest for the health of her community. She found another way forward and moved the community to Dubuque.[5]

This was a painful choice for Mother Xavier. Yet, Jesus leaves open the option of "shaking the dust from your feet and moving on" (Matt 10:14) for her and for us. When do we remain in relationship and when do we shake the dust from our feet and move on? Mother Xavier made the choice to move in order to safeguard her fledgling community. Moving on was a matter of survival and finding a space in a neighboring diocese in which the community could share its charism and thrive. She created possibilities and new

[5] The story of the early history of the Sisters of St. Francis of Dubuque is found in *They Have Taken Root: The Sisters of the Third Order of St. Francis of the Holy Family* by Mary Eunice Mousel (New York: Bookman Associates, 1954).

life by moving on and not continuing to allow clergy to deplete her resources—financial, spiritual, and emotional.

- How do we know when it's time to shake the dust from our feet and move on?

- What are the consequences of moving on?

- What helps us to create possibilities and new life in seemingly impossible circumstances?

Sister Phyllis Vaske – An Unexpected Connection

Support can come to us from unexpected places. When I was involved in parish ministry in the most difficult clergy situation I have faced, a number of my sisters gathered for an area group meeting. Every sister in my community belonged to an area group, largely based on geographical regions. Participation in area groups was a way to deepen relationships across the community as well as engage in the business of the congregation. When the nineteen sisters from my area group gathered, the last sister I expected to connect with over painful clergy experiences was Sister Phyllis Vaske. I admit that I made that judgment based on appearances. Phyllis was the only sister in my area group who wore a veil. Based on that alone, I concluded that she would be more defensive of the clergy than understanding toward my experiences. I couldn't have been more wrong.

After I had shared my current struggles with clerical abuses, Phyllis came and found me. With red-rimmed eyes she told me that she was working for an abusive pastor. She didn't use the word "abuse" to describe her experiences. However, her voice cracked as she told me about the pastor who yelled at her, manipulated her, and treated her disgracefully. I sensed her shock that this was happening to her. We promised to pray for each other, and we sent each other supportive emails after that exchange.

I remain grateful for the gift of Phyllis's vulnerability in sharing her story with me. She taught me that my suppositions based on appearance could be completely wrong. She also taught me that abuses by clergy are far more pervasive than I had considered. Phyllis's sharing also convinced me that my entire community supported me—even though many were unaware of what I was facing. Phyllis taught me to expect support, understanding, and wise advice from all of my sisters.

When I was in the midst of an oppressive church situation (and ultimately reported a priest for abusive behavior), my spiritual director checked with me each month:

- When is it time to get out? I didn't have to remain. I could leave at any time.

- Was it becoming too unhealthy for me to remain in the situation?

- How would I know if it was time to leave?

I was aware that I could leave at any time. However, the single mothers who also worked at the parish did not have the same support and flexibility that I had. I decided that remaining until I had enough undisputed evidence to report the priest was something I could do for others. I also realized that as long as I found creative options within the situation, I was okay enough to remain.

- So, are we listlessly going with the flow? Have we numbed ourselves to the pain in our relationship with the church? (If we have, are we good for anyone?)

- Where do we find creative options? Where is the new life? Where is the possibility?

- When have you encountered unexpected support? How did it empower and strengthen you?

Sistering the Church

So, I return to the question: What does it mean for me to be in right relationship with the clergy in the Catholic Church? The answer is embedded in my vows. Celibacy has made me a sister to all. This is my touchstone when I am trying to discern how I should respond in any challenging situation. But what does it mean to be not only a sister *in* the church, but also a sister *to* the church? There are many different ways of being a sister. A big sister may play an entirely different role within the family dynamics than a little sister or even a twin sister.

As a Big Sister

A big sister, at her best, is a leader and sometimes even another mother to her siblings. In this capacity she is attentive to including everyone, making sure everyone has what they need (if not what they want), and protecting the vulnerable. Big sisters (especially if they are the oldest child in the family) are likely rule followers at heart, expecting that the existing structures of the family and society are there to provide support and promote the common good. They want the systems to work fairly. However, when systems are not working, when younger siblings are harmed, a big sister can become a fierce protector and advocate. When younger siblings are failing to behave appropriately, a big sister will correct the behavior. No doubt, this is where the idea of a "bossy older sister" comes from.

Jesus compares himself to a mother hen as he laments the coming destruction of Jerusalem when he says, "I yearned to gather your children together, as a hen gathers her young under her wings (Matt 23:37)." This image encapsulates the big sister who desires to protectively gather chicks under her wing. Sister Pat Farrell, in her presidential address to LCWR during the Vatican's investigation of LCWR, also invokes the image of sisters acting in a protective role as she notes that: "A lightning rod draws the charge to itself, channels and grounds it, providing protection. A lightning rod doesn't hold onto the destructive energy but allows it to flow into the earth to be transformed."[6]

A big sister may also have the courage to say the uncomfortable truth that no one wants to hear. She may point out that which is unjust or unfair in the church—perhaps by noting that women are relegated to a second-class status within the church. However, if she doesn't speak up on behalf of herself, she may be even more likely to make people uncomfortable for the sake of others. For example, if women are second-class citizens, then our LGBTQ+ siblings in Christ are too often condemned and treated as if there is no room at all for them within our church.

In her 2018 address to the USCCB, Sister Teresa Maya epitomizes the big sister role as she challenges the bishops: "Look to your left and to your right—the men of the church need the women of the church to re-create our Catholic Communion."[7] With gentleness, humility, and an acknowledgment that sisters also fail at times, Teresa challenges the USCCB to consider: "Could it be that some of our structures are no longer relevant in a renewing and vibrant Church? . . . Could it be that we must recognize our failure to care for the core and to trust that a new tree will grow with God's grace?"

---

[6] Pat Farrell, OSF, "Navigating the Shifts" (presidential address, LCWR Assembly, 2012).

[7] Teresa Maya, CCVI, "USCCB Called to Communion" (address, USCCB General Assembly, November 2018). Of course, the Franciscans are not the *only* sources of wisdom in my life. CCVIs (like Tere Maya) and many others inspire me as well. However, I have primarily relied on Franciscans in negotiating my relationship with the hierarchical structure of the church.

When acting as a big sister to the church, sisters may be called to point out when things are not happening as they should. Sisters are among the most educated women in the church (though many of our lay sisters have joined us as well). Sometimes we are more educated than our brother clergy. We are more than qualified by life experience devoted to the people on the margins, as well as theological education, to provide big sisterly feedback. We can step into our role with grace.

As a Little Sister

If the older sister is a rule follower, the younger sister often was not raised with the same rules as older children in the family. The younger sister may have been perceived by older siblings as having gotten away with everything. Younger sisters often benefit from the more relaxed parenting styles of more experienced (or just plain tired) parents. Younger sisters may be the doted upon darlings in the family, receiving an outpouring of affection. As a result, they may be confident and comfortable discerning that the rules do not always apply to them. They may be more flexible than older sisters. Little sisters also know how to be pesky until they get their way—which may not always be such a bad thing.

The little sister may be less directly threatening, as she wasn't an authority figure within the family. She might have a gentler way of encouraging people along. (Big sisters are not all as gentle as Teresa Maya is in the example above.) The things my youngest sister can say to my father still surprise me.

Anything less than loving inclusion of people wherever they are is not likely to be tolerated by a little sister at her best. There is a great gift in the confidence of being well-loved beyond the rules that may help point to a way forward in the church. The Gospel image that comes to mind is that of Jesus picking grain on the Sabbath (Matt 12:1-8). People need nourishing. Stopping to consider any rules external to the fact that people need nourishment seems superfluous to the younger sister beyond "the rules." If the hierarchy of the church is not supportive of people, a little sister will have an easier time shaking the dust from her feet, shrugging her shoulders, and moving on—after she picks all the grain she needs, of course. Even though less directly confrontational, it may be the most threatening position within the church.

This may be why so many clergy fail to understand women religious. We may have maintained the barest of relationships, but we've also moved on. We don't pour our energy into a dysfunctional, energy-draining system that has little to no room for the perspectives of women. Instead, we've carved out alternative spaces for prayer and spirituality for ourselves and others. I cannot count the number of times people have admitted to me that they are connected to women's religious communities, but are no longer interested in the larger Catholic Church.

As a Twin Sister

A twin sister is a partner, an automatic companion, in everything growing up—from learning to discovering trouble. The twin toddlers in my family seem to understand each other when no one else has a clue what they are saying. They move in opposite directions and complement each other's gifts. One twin is outgoing, while one is a little more reticent. One can't sit still, while the other can concentrate and play alone for a while. The twins learn new words and discover new forms of trouble by watching each other. They are also incredibly tolerant of each other. One can wake up screaming from naptime, and the other will sleep right through it. They each have their roles within their twin relationship. It's one twin's job to test the waters, to meet new people first, and to give quick, fierce hugs. It's the other twin's job to snuggle in grandma's lap, to observe, to figure out what's going on and sometimes make decisions for both of them. The twins allow each other to use their personalities and natural gifts in a way that benefits them both.

A twin sister to the church must be a partner in growth and collaboration. Being a sibling implies equality. However, operating as a twin sister emphasizes and insists upon equality within the church. Even though twins complement each other, I am by no means suggesting "complementarity," insofar as leadership is considered a gift associated with men, and women are relegated to the role of nurturing helper. I deliberately chose not to identify gender when describing the roles of the twins in my family. Roles should be determined by God-given personalities and gifts—not gender. Instead, a twin sister relationship with the church means a functioning partnership, where gifts are recognized, celebrated, and utilized for the sake of the people of God.

The synodal process is teaching the church to listen to the wisdom of everyone in order to consider a path forward together as a church. If we become listeners and decisions are made through contemplative listening for the guidance of the Holy Spirit in our midst, we are operating as twin sisters.

There is no one answer that determines what it means to be in right relationship with the hierarchical structure of the church. It takes an entire community of Franciscan saints to guide me! Similarly, I would suggest that it is advantageous to consider that different times and situations may call forth different ways of being sister from us. It may be most appropriate to act as the big sister, the little sister, or a twin sister, depending on the situation.

- When are you called to be a big sister, little sister, or twin sister in your relationship with the church?

- Which type of sister do you resonate with most, and why?

- Are there additional characteristics of big, little, or twin sisters that may enhance your understanding of what it means to be in right relationship with the church?

- Who are your community of saints who support your discernment?

5

Soul Sisters from Yonder

Chioma Ahanihu, SLW

Introduction

Human beings continue to evolve, and the process of this movement leads us to wonder, to what end? People leave their country of birth, state of origin, and communities for another place for different reasons. We look around the world and see that immigration, or crossing borders, is still a big part of what's going on in the world today. This movement can be scripturally related to the Abrahamic mandate: "Depart from your land, and from your kindred, and from your father's house, and come into the land that I will show you" (Gen 12:1). While this is a mandate to Abraham from God, people are compelled to leave from their natural-born native lands to other areas due to many reasons. It could be seeking better economic opportunities, escaping political oppression, displacement due to unrest, personal/familial choice, and so on.

Consecrated women in the Catholic Church today have not been left out of this movement. Sisters are part of this migration, either as fully professed sisters or as young women who moved on their own or with their families and then received a call to the religious vocation in their new country. This essay will discuss the blessings and struggles of women in consecrated life who have migrated to the United States and become members of religious orders.

The beauty of religious life is the diversity of members—diverse in age, nationality, and ethnic or cultural upbringing. I, for one, will count myself as a part of this diversity. I see myself as an immigrant who lives in two worlds—in the world of my country of birth, with my biological family in Nigeria, and in my newfound world, with my religious community in the United States. I operate within these two worlds daily. There are also many other consecrated women and men who are in the same space with me. The word *transnationalism* comes to mind as I think of myself and my sisters who occupy this space. "Transnationalism among migrants, however, does not only concern networks and exchanges of goods but also transnational religious practices that involve the transformation of identity, community, and ritual practices."[1]

These sisters, as they become a part of their new communities, share their cultural heritage with their sisters, who most often are ready to accept and learn from them. From my research, some of these sisters have migrated to the United States with their families or alone, and in this process, the desire arises to be in consecrated life as a woman religious. They heed the call with their commitment of *yes* to God who has called them.

The Emergence of Global Migrant Sisters

I began to observe the trend of the emergence of what I call the Global Migrant Sisters (GMS) through my re-

[1] Dominic Pasura and Marta Bivand Erdal, eds., *Migration, Transnationalism and Catholicism: Global Perspectives* (London: Palgrave Macmillan, 2017), 24.

search work and in friendships and relationships developed among us in Giving Voice (GV). GV is a network of younger women religious from different religious congregations in the US who are under the age of fifty. There is a growing number of GMS, sisters who were born in countries outside of the United States, joining religious life in the US. I refer to these women as the Global Migrant Sisters because they are transnationals, immigrants, and members of different religious congregations in the United States. In the book *New Faces, New Possibilities*, the Center for Applied Research in the Apostolate (CARA) recorded that at least "one in five new members of women's institutes was born in a country other than the United States."[2] Respondents to the CARA survey came from sixty-eight countries.

My interest in this group of women increased when I began to encounter many of us who fall under this category in our Giving Voice meetings. This goes to show that while the world continues to experience migration in various places, not even the consecrated life is left out of that experience. For example, at our annual retreat gathering a few years ago, we realized that in a group of sixteen younger sisters present for the retreat, twelve of us were born and lived the first quarter of our lives outside of the US. This was a visible sign of a transformation taking place in consecrated life today.

The Blessings of Global Migrant Sisters

These transnational women religious bring with them so many gifts that each of them share with sisters they live with in community, in their ministry, and with the world

---

[2] Center for Applied Research in the Apostolate, *New Faces, New Possibilities: Cultural Diversity and Structural Change in Institutes of Women Religious*, ed. Thomas P. Gaunt and Thu T. Do (Collegeville, MN: Liturgical Press, 2022), 7.

at large. Migrants "move with who they are, their biological upbringing, cultural heritages and ideologies which they donate and express in their receiving communities."[3] We bring the gift of speaking and understanding many languages, which is a highly needed gift in American society, given its increasing diversity. A sister friend of mine shared that she was in a situation in her ministry where she was called upon to translate for a woman in a care facility who could not speak English. It was becoming difficult for her to get her needs met by the care providers. Without that translation support in a different language, this woman might not have received the appropriate health services she needed. One might ask, "what about her family?" Sometimes translation by a third person is preferred, especially in adult care issues. Hence, the sister was able to provide translation services for this patient because she understands her language.

GMS sisters also bring the gifts of adaptability, ability to live a diverse way of life, assimilation, and accommodation of new people, culture, food, and places. Given the nature of the reasons for these sisters' transition to another country and culture altogether, their ability to adapt to their new environment and thrive shows their tenacity to withstand the shock and difficulties experienced by immigrants in new places. The fact that they adapted and were able to join a religious congregation in the United States gives hope to the sustainability of religious life, given the receding nature of America-born religious entrants.

While this process and relationship might not be smooth at the beginning, as some of my sister friends have shared, the receiving sisters in community with the GMS also have a role to play by accepting and accommodating

[3] Pasura and Erdal, *Migration, Transnationalism and Catholicism*, 29.

their new companions with their gifts and talents. The receiving sisters are mandated in love to accept these newer and younger women as part of their community, and to help them assimilate into the life of a consecrated woman in United States. The younger sisters tell their stories as immigrants who have left their home country for a foreign place and met their sisters with whom they share the love and joys of religious life. They tell stories of what sacrifices and lessons they go through in their communal living, especially when they share communal life with sisters in another age bracket or who also have different ethnic origins from them. And yet they share so much joy, despite their differences in age, race, ethnic upbringing, and life stories. They learn to live in joy through sharing who they are and being listened to as sojourners of faith and as sister sojourners together.

These two groups of sisters—GMS and receiving sisters—experience a vulnerability that can only be accommodated by the love of Christ who has called them into this life. The receiving countries and communities sometimes struggle with welcoming immigrants. They may not see the gifts that our immigrant sisters bring, but focus instead on immigration status, which is only a minor part of who we are. The consecrated life mandates us, while human, to live beyond the present struggle, to be an example for the world that embraces all as one in Christ. These are the joys and hopes that consecrated religious, both women and men, are called to witness in our time today.

This is the reseeding work that we are all called to be part of, and to live in, as we share the same body and blood of Christ and witness to the world in our answer to that vocational call, our response of *yes* to God in love. These are the blessings that GMS help us to see: that as we live in abundance, we have what we need to share in the one life as consecrated religious. We cannot live in fear of the vulnerability that intercultural, intergenerational communal living poses for us. Rather, we must live in the joy of the Gospel of Christ, who has loved us abundantly and equally.

New Hope in Our Midst

While these joys of the GMS bring hope in religious life, many questions arise out of my curiosity about the sustainability of religious life, especially in the United States. What is ours to do as religious women in America today? What do the GMS have to offer their receiving congregations here in the United States? Statistically, many categorized as minorities in US American religious communities are black and brown sisters (as evidenced from the Giving Voice retreat gathering experience I mentioned above). How is this current trend shaping religious life in the United States? What effects do communal living have on both the giving sisters (migrants) and receiving sisters (hosts) in response to their religious vocation? As fewer white Americans opt for membership in religious congregations, how do these younger sisters of color (transnationals) assimilate, cope, and adjust to their newfound home as immigrant sisters? How can this shift the way we think? How might the movement of sisters around the world strengthen, grow, and deepen our bonds as people who have chosen this path of life and live it in joy? Of course, God is doing something new! I hope we see it, and I hope that we are curious to witness it. Consecrated life as we know it is transforming. The world is changing in this global movement.

I see the GMS trend as a gift to our church, especially our church in America. We are answering the question of the possible ways in which congregations can engage and seize this moment as an opportunity to reshape our lives, spirituality, and understanding of the global church. The global church in itself is a pilgrim church, because where Christians are, there is the church. The global movement of Christians is also the global movement of the church. The church has never been static, and so we as consecrated women and men cannot be static in our ways. We have to look at the signs of the time, accept and embrace our new realities, and flourish in them. We need to be aware that while we have our charism to live by, we also have a common charism of religious life that inspires us to keep going and keep giving in love. Sister Rosemary Nassif observes that "there is a charism—a spirit—an animation alive within our global sisterhood, just as there are many charisms within our congregations. We need to pay attention to that charism as we pay attention to our own."[4]

Of the "Coming to Completion" Process

Another trend that I have witnessed, as I continue to joyously respond to my call in this beautiful life as a religious woman, is the dynamic shift caused by fewer numbers of entrants into religious life. Some religious congregations, more of women than of men, are choosing to go through the process of "coming to completion" due to their reduced number, and in answering the question of their viability and sustainability at this time. Congregations that are contemplating or actively have begun this path are carrying it out in different ways, given their uniqueness and their needs.

[4] Rosemary Nassif, "Supporting the Emergence of Global Sisterhood" (presentation, Plenary Assembly of International Union of Superiors General, Rome, Italy, 2016), 4.

While this trend historically is not a new one in the church or in consecrated life, what makes this time different is the continued embrace of the blessings and joys we younger religious bring to this process of completion, while living out our *yes*! This way of life is by all means counter-cultural in our world today, where commitment continues to be a big question mark for the younger population. That these global sisters, who could have chosen different paths of life other than entering religious communities that are choosing to "complete," are still interested in their communities is what I call the "golden gift" to religious life of today.

Indeed, religious life is undergoing a transformation. This is what I call God using what ordinarily would have been dead in creating and making new life. We do not own our lives, and I believe that my journey without God is completely useless. That keeps me going every day, coupled with the knowledge that God knows what God is about in the lives of consecrated women and men, and so we only do our part.

We live our lives in full uncertainty of what tomorrow brings. Who knows what tomorrow brings, even when our lives are assured? I have continued to find fulfillment and have encountered my sisters and myself living out our lives in so much joy and in collaboration, as if there is no tomorrow! We live our lives as vessels ready for our Love to use us as he pleases. I believe that there is no vessel that God has set on fire that God does not call the world to watch as it blossoms, and so it is with our lives, lived as a witness among all. I talk with my elderly sisters in the nursing home, and the encouragement I receive from them gives me hope that I am in the right place.

We, the younger and middle-aged sisters, have gone beyond the knowledge that we are in transition. We have begun to collaborate more in our ministries and in communal living spaces across congregations. I believe we are experiencing a transformational time in our church and in our consecrated life. Hence, while coming to completion is a reality for some congregations, the sisters involved must live out their lives in the joy of the Gospel as they answer their call to religious life. I understand from my studies in social work that times of transformation can be painful, while as a practical theologian, the hope and trust in God gives me the grace of the day to continue to say yes to the call and live in abundance.

Conclusion

This global sisterhood, the transnational religious women who bring color and flare to today's consecrated life, is a confirmation of God's attunement to the consecrated life of today. God is still at work. We need to learn what is ours to do, and to do it. It does not matter when one is called to this life. What matters is how one answers this call in their time. I encourage us all to pay attention to the Spirit of God in the new life God brings to us in our communities, and to nurture it for our future as consecrated people of God.

6

Reseeding in Scorched Ground: Reclaiming My Vocation to Religious Life

Ricca Dimalibot, CCVI

I agreed to write this essay in hopes of reclaiming why I choose to stay in religious life and snap out of secretly plotting to get away. Streaming my thoughts to my fingertips stirs up solace and dread, convincing me to discern this, cede control, and yield to where it leads me. I admit that, in some ways, I have brought myself to these crossroads through my own dysfunction; I've allowed a productivity-obsessed ministry in medicine to hemorrhage into how I live religious life. My Filipino culture, which values family obligations, filial duty, hard work and obedience, has also influenced my decisions, directing my experiences in religious and professional life in subtle yet powerful ways. This inflection point hasn't come out of left field; it has been decades in the making. Twenty-four years in religious life, now in the yoke of leadership for my congregation, and more than three decades in the medical profession are finally catching up to me. It pains me to explore how I became someone I didn't intend to be. How did I get here?

Never once have I been asked why I remain a sister, though I've been asked a hundred different ways why I became one. The latter question has always been easy to answer. The former—at least these days—needs more nuanced pondering. To be in a significant relationship means realizing that the journey is not always easy, and commitment requires a daily affirmation to live the promise consciously and intentionally. Those passionate enough would entertain doubt at least once in their lifetime and inevitably start questioning their choices; each iteration of the answer validates and strengthens one's conviction.

When I decided to enter religious life in 1999, I was undoubtedly on a dopamine high and oxytocin boost, wiring my brain to be utterly in love with Jesus. I felt the call to share in Jesus' life more genuinely. When I was young, I thought that was only possible after death, and that the drama-free afterlife might be dull. Through a prayerful path, I soon became aware that God was always within me and relentlessly inviting me, and that I needed only to open my heart to God's grace. No course in life could compare to the pursuit of intimacy and participation in the inner life of God. I desperately wanted to plant my feet firmly in the very ground of God's being. Convinced that the sisters might be on to something, I decided to join them.

I have always been in awe of God's love manifested through the lives of all our brothers and sisters who preceded me in consecrated life. My aunt, who was a member of the Daughters of St. Paul, inspired me with what I could only describe as spiritual imprinting through her joy-filled presence whenever our family visited her at her convent once a year. Still today, gratitude and respect overwhelm me as I realize anew that I stand on the shoulders of my foremothers, who paved the way for me and continue to accompany me in my quest for the ultimate. The sacrifices of women and men who dedicated their lives to God through the priesthood and religious life for centuries laid the bedrock of selfless service for those living on the margins of society. Religious institutes built and fully staffed hospitals, parishes, schools, soup kitchens, and countless other ministries. They are on the frontlines of advocating for social justice, openly voicing their discontent with patriarchy and misogyny, trailblazing to champion equality, and even putting their lives on the line. I knew it was a high calling, a tough act to follow, especially when the expectation of the church at large was so high.

Twice in my life, I ventured to leave everything behind. In pursuing my professional ambition in medicine, I left my home country in my early twenties. My memories were packed in two suitcases, with only a few dollars in my pocket. I was going to be a doctor in the United States, mainly because it was expected of me by my family, but also because I was looking forward to being a part of the healing profession. When I heeded the call to a religious vocation in my early thirties, I had intended to leave medicine completely. That idea only lasted a couple of years before I went back to practicing again. It turned out that God had more in store for me through this ministry.

My hours were grueling in my practice at a family medicine clinic for the underserved and uninsured in the suburbs of Houston. Still, like my religious vocation, I knew I was where I was supposed to be. Medicine became the preeminent path to my full discovery of a life of service. Practicing medicine provided professional fulfillment with no ounce of unspent energy to spare. I grew spiritually as I learned compassion and empathy from my patients and aspired to follow Jesus Christ, the consummate healer. I sensed the pulse of the community around me, more than any textbook or artificial intelligence algorithm could teach me, while being immersed in the vulnerability I witnessed in my patients. In the exam room, I put aside my circuitous introspection and meaningfully entered the space of unguarded encounters with the other. I also stepped away to walk on the "other side" and gleaned wisdom from people going through interminable adversity and poverty. No one with a front seat to the atrocities of cancer, ravages of mental illness, debility caused by violence, or the miracle of life could remain unchanged. Medicine humbled me profoundly, constantly reminding me of my mortality and dependence on God. The tough hours, the painstaking attention to detail, the endless study to keep up with new evidence-based information, and the challenge of managing staff and personalities prepared me for my role in congregational leadership. While the new work demands of my congregation have required me to drastically decrease my clinic hours, after five years in the role, I'm finding that the pressure of constant availability for both medicine and religious life is untenable, even harmful.

Lately, I have become more cynical, little things irritate me, and my tasks feel like drudgery. Jesus' words, "I have come to set fire on the earth," used to inspire me, but now make me cringe as I ruminate over another item on my bottomless to-do list. Guilt creeps in when I am not working, causing me to spend less and less time with friends and family. My laptop, cell phone, health tracker, and watch, on the other hand, never leave me alone. They feel like leeches sucking the life out of me. Is this what burnout looks like?

My ideals about medicine have also taken a battering. Cracks and systemic inefficiencies in healthcare were obvious even before the COVID-19 pandemic, but the effects have multiplied and magnified, leading many workers to experience burnout: "[A] syndrome conceptualized as resulting from chronic workplace stress that has not been successfully managed. It is characterized by three dimensions: feelings of energy depletion or exhaustion; increased mental distance from one's job, or feelings of negativism or cynicism related to one's job; and reduced professional efficacy."[1] In a world obsessed with efficiency and precision, no profession is exempt from facing the brunt of burnout.

Among those in the medical field, many argue that burnout does not adequately capture reality because compassion, resiliency, and ambition mask the gravity of the problem. We have all benefited from the around-the-clock work shifts and holiday schedules that have kept our world from being a sicker place. We forget that novel medical breakthroughs and advances fueled by arduous hours of service and research levied a personal toll on countless workers. Many of us in healthcare often bear the weight of the responsibility to address a patient's affliction and do something about it. As the work demands in medicine pile up, so do the missed birthdays, anniversaries, and important life milestones of healthcare workers caring for others. It still haunts me that I was not at my parents' hospital bedsides when they took their last breaths.

While the signs are all there, I still wonder if I am experiencing burnout when I will to believe in the meaning and purpose of serving God, despite the unrelenting bid for my time. Can it really be compassion fatigue when personal touch and conversations with people around me still have the ability to nourish and sustain me? As opposed to burnout, what seems to resonate with many of my colleagues and me is the idea of moral injury, which has been described as "potentially morally injurious events, such as perpetrating, failing to prevent, or bearing witness to acts

[1] World Health Organization, *International Classification of Diseases*, 11th Revision (Geneva: World Health Organization, 2018), https://icd.who.int/browse11/l-m/en.

that transgress deeply held moral beliefs and expectations may be deleterious in the long-term, emotionally, psychologically, behaviorally, spiritually, and socially."[2] Perhaps it is not only about the incredible work demands but rather decades of witnessing unnecessary physical suffering amid a system that often appears to undermine the most prudent course of action for our brothers and sisters in grave situations. Perhaps the years of repetitive stress on my moral values have sickened my conscience and frayed the grain of my faith. Healthcare workers are prone to a pervasive feeling of helplessness when they want to bring about cure and healing but are restricted by insufficient access to resources. I am painfully aware of my participation in perpetuating the inequality that is endemic in my profession. The medical profession, a field I cherish and to which I have dedicated more than half of my life, was meant to express God's healing and wholeness. However, it has morphed into a structure that exhausts and disheartens me, as I find myself inadvertently enabling its broken system.

Could the same moral injury I'm facing in my ministry spill over into how I am experiencing religious life at this point? I've felt for a while that my wounds from healthcare may be preventing me from fully realizing who God meant me to be as a sister. What if the demands of my ministry have become a barrier to God's personal call, drowned out by the incessant busyness of my tasks? When I entered religious life, I never imagined spending extensive hours in administrative responsibilities and assuming a role more akin to a business executive than a pastoral companion. I belong to an international congregation and am involved in a fair amount of administrative governance, legal super-

---

[2] Brett T. Litz and others, "Moral Injury and Moral Repair in War Veterans: A Preliminary Model and Intervention Strategy," *Clinical Psychology Review*, vol. 29, no. 8 (December 2009): 695–706.

vision, and financial oversight, all of which are critical to keeping the congregation's mission alive. Learning about investments, participating in boards, and property management are crucial in keeping the practical side of our charism. However, I never thought it would consume so many of my waking hours. Work–life balance is a myth for me. We have enough administrative staff and several organizations are ready to help us, yet so much work remains. There are moments when I feel unequipped to handle these matters because they are not in my line of competence or interest, yet I understand they must be done in the name of serving the greater good.

I am profoundly grateful for the tremendous work of the sisters who came before me and had the foresight to ensure our viability and sustainability. Because of them, undertaking the background administrative work we are doing now allows our institute to expand its reach by partnering with like-minded groups serving the poor and marginalized worldwide. It is never a question of my willingness to assume my responsibilities and commitments for my ministry and congregation, because I am prepared to do anything that will lead to the blossoming of our lives as sisters in Christ and the blossoming of the lives of those we serve.

I am aware that I cannot live in a world of what-ifs. Every sister has a different perspective, and I cannot generalize my experience. My personality, culture, and how I choose to respond to what is in front of me also contribute to the tight corner I find myself in. The medical training that instinctively compels me to look for problems and worst-case scenarios makes my situation more incorrigible. It doesn't help that while slaving and making all kinds of plans, I've also made myself accustomed to the comforts of middle-class life, of not having to worry about my next meal, where I will sleep, my vacations, my healthcare needs, my retirement, and even my final resting place. We live in a consumerist society and I find myself easily seduced by its immediate rewards and expectations.

There is often an idealistic side to individuals who take the path of priesthood and religious life. In many ways, that makes it harder when the realities of racism, abuse, addiction, manipulation, and so forth arise in community life. Even with the best intentions to live in God's service, some of us become complicit in blocking the flow of God's grace instead of being conduits of mercy to people who are in need. I ask myself whether I am also a part of the culture that sometimes engenders spiritual malaise, denial, inattentiveness to the core of our life, misfocus on the mission, and tepid community living. Adding to the burden of my heart are the frequent talks of diminishment, completion, and dissatisfaction. I also seem to take rather heavily the numerous scandals and crises plaguing the church and the dwindling beliefs of so many. These cause me to ask if these attitudes are the symptoms of an institutional framework subtly molding its members into lives incongruent with their true calling. Many of us entered religious life aspiring to fulfill our deepest desires through a way of life receptive to the Holy Spirit's guidance, where we have the greatest support to grow spiritually and pursue the means to unite ourselves wholeheartedly with the people of God in both suffering and joy. When I became a doctor, I dreamed of positively impacting the health and well-being of my patients. What happens when the structures where we align ourselves frustrate that purpose and become the system that quenches our fervor because of inflexible rules rather than embodying love and mercy? Instead of institutions being shaped by individuals as havens for flourishing in the service of the greater good, the framework often lulls its members into complacency, masquerading good works done in its name, with thousands benefiting from its ministries.

Institutions that keep doing the same unanimated things will become stagnant containers that no longer achieve the purpose of serving their members, but instead become potent breeding grounds of dysfunctional attitudes, woefully leading to the distortion of our Christian faith. The questions arise: How might we mold and reshape institutions and challenge them to align and support our true vocation rather than the reverse? What would it take to challenge and transform these foundations into structures solely dedicated to fostering the walls and beams supporting faithful living in their pursuit of love, who is God? Perhaps in such a realm we would have chosen the better part.

Leaders are tasked with keeping God's vision alive for religious life, an endeavor that is easier said than done when we are too preoccupied with maintaining and surviving. In trying to keep the infrastructure of our institutes intact, are we failing in our witness to the Gospel in the way we live our lives? On the other hand, could I be using the administrative burdens and the self-imposed keeping up with the past successes of ministries and the roles of my predecessors as my excuses for not hearing what God is asking me to do? What if we creatively find ways to reappropriate our accumulated means and resources? Pope Francis repeatedly emphasizes the culture of encounter by going to the margins, listening to the people, and being in solidarity with the masses. He says the church gets rusty when it becomes a club of nice people who do religious duties but lack the courage to get out to the peripheries.[3] How can I "smell like

[3] *The Pope: Answers*, directed by Jordi Évole and Marius Sánchez (2003).

the sheep" if I'm always close to the center of my protected environment?

This growing restlessness on two fronts—medicine and religious life—is discouraging and might be too much for me to hold. I despair at the prospect of not fully realizing who I am as a doctor and a leader in religious life because of the small box I have built around me to conform to what I am expected to do and how I am supposed to act. How do I respond in a way that honors the authentic truths about who I am in God's eyes? I know I need to rise above the deluge of worldly pressures; otherwise, my vows will be in vain if I fail to read the signs and discover the deeper meaning of God's message through all these experiences.

While discussing my quandary with my spiritual director, I told him that our faith sometimes works against us because it inflates what we think we can accomplish. He quickly retorted, "That's not faith if you have to justify it and have the expectation to succeed." He gently told me that not much of what we do is likely to matter in the long run except as a source of love to a world much in need of love. What is done in love may have consequences far beyond what we perceive. Time and time again, he reminds me that my reason for doing my ministry and to whom I am offering it sanctifies it, that my work is holy. It is no longer *mere* work, but a sacred act that God has gifted me to benefit the world. My work could be one of my spiritual paths, contemplation in action. No matter how tedious the endless paperwork, meetings, and Zoom calls, what I am doing now expresses anew our congregation's mission and how we serve the world as we listen to its needs with our foundational call as our guide.

I've asked myself several times, "How do I remain faithful in living the very essence of religious life through all the anxiety, busyness, and uncertainty right before me?" I've had many conversations regarding this topic with sisters from different congregations, and many of us talk through the unsettling future of our way of life. Deep in our hearts, we know that our charisms and religious life will surely endure, even if our memory and legacy take on a different form. We know that charism is not *our* possession, but rather is the Holy Spirit's gift to the world. Our co-ministers, associates, and benefactors possess the same charism and caught it directly from the same Spirit that caught us; we did not hand it to them as we're prone to imagine. There is enough space for all of us to work together and serve the same purpose and mission.

Wishful thinking is never a good game plan regardless of the vastness of my faith; I must go through a transformation of the heart and be intentional in discerning the emerging future of religious life for my call to survive. Jesus reminds me that he is the Sower and the seed in our universe primed for reseeding. Even the seeds that fell on the path and were eaten by the birds served the noble purpose of providing nourishment, and the seeds that fell on rocky ground and burned up when the sun rose eventually fertilized the ground to bring forth new life (Matt 13:24-33). Religious congregations are like the mustard seed that the sower sows and "birds of the sky come and dwell in its branches," a full disclosure of God's reckless mercy. We are the mustard plant that is sufficiently nourished by taking only what is needed, trusting that the rich soil will provide everything for us to grow, accomplishing our purpose in due time, and not outliving what we are meant to be according to God's design. The new members are not replacements for all the sisters who have gone before us but are the new seeds that will grow and have their own fruits through God's nurturing and caring. Religious institutes have a historical beginning, and many will reach fulfillment during our lifetime. We were breathed into existence by God, who loves us unconditionally. We will exist until God's appointed time for us in history. Anything beyond is setting limits on the power of God. Ultimately, we will end where we began—in the heart of God.

There is freedom in conceding that the future of religious life is beyond our vision and imagination, no matter how beautiful they are. I want to believe that the essence of religious life is not a construct of our numbers, ministries, or identity. Our mission is not based on age and our numbers will always be enough. I believe that what I have dedicated my life to still has much to say to the world. Who we are and what we do in the global public square touches lives and makes a difference. The spiritual space of diversity and inclusion we create through our global sisterhood permeates the world like a smoldering wick of love and divine energy. God's vision for religious life is within and among us; our consecration anointed us to be seized by that grace and be Christ to the world.

I unite my voice with all my brothers and sisters who envision becoming bold, prophetic witnesses of the Word who became flesh and pitched his tent among us to relate to our humanity. I desire to be one with religious communities around the globe that strive to be places of communion with God through wide open doors and porous borders that create fertile ground to plant new seeds. I am in awe of the generosity of the seed that gave up its life to bring new life that sparks a mystical journey, a path where God will always find us fully alive! When we heed the summons for a remolding and recasting of our consciousness, we reorient our mindset and recognize to whom our congregations have always belonged and where we have forever existed in the mind of God. We are indeed in this together, and together is the only way to go. Yet, it wouldn't hurt if, from time to time, some of us would jump and forego the safety of the boat like Peter; we may temporarily sink but at least we risked being safe for a chance to walk on water and ascend to a new level of relationship while touching the hand of Jesus pulling us out of the water (Matt 14:22-33). I hear an invitation to dare ourselves to leap over the narrow walls of our silos and allow ourselves to be instruments of God's grace for the sake of *the Life*!

For the umpteenth time, Jesus reminds me that I should not settle for something less than who I truly am—the beloved daughter of God. No matter how long my to-do list may seem, there will never come a time when it's a good idea to hide inside a bushel. I stay because I believe that in my dis-ease, Jesus is firmly holding on to me, prompting me to be an extension of his compassion and mercy. Amid the exhaustion, conflicts, obligations, burnout, and moral wounds, Jesus asks me to lend myself the same kindness I give to the people I serve. I remain faithful to my vows because I know that it is only in sharing my wound and touching the wound of Jesus by offering my life entirely to him that I will begin to see the wounds of the world and be part of its healing. The ache I am going through is Jesus leading me to an intense emptiness until I have nowhere else to go but trace the ultimate source of all sustenance to awaken a much deeper yearning—the Beloved seeking union with me. The hunger becomes all-consuming in the stillness of nothingness until I hear his voice quickening from within me and I finally surrender to the immensity of his incomprehensible, radical love. Leaning into the Holy Spirit's beckoning through the unbroken call we share with our foremothers, we till the ground where the new seeds will grow and have everything we need for the flourishing of religious life.

7

We Need One Another

Juliet Mousseau, RSCJ

When I entered the Society of the Sacred Heart in 2009, I didn't really know what I was in for. I definitely knew that I was called, that God had written something into my heart, and that the something I felt called to do was somehow going to be answered in this congregation. I knew that I felt at home, at peace, and excited about the future. I also knew that my own life was on the verge of a giant change. I moved into a community of seven, in which I was younger than anyone else by more than half. I was thirty—not a child in the non-convent world. Most of my friends had long ago married, and most already had children.

One thing I didn't know at the time was how much religious life would help me grow into the person God called me to be. I didn't know that all the trauma and pain of my own childhood would come marching back to affect my new relationships with sisters. I didn't know that I would receive the extraordinary support and love to face my own past pain in order to learn from it, heal from it, and move forward with healthier relationships. I didn't know how much formation as a sister would bring me wholeness and happiness.

What I also didn't know was the rapidity of change I would see in the congregation. When I entered, we were over three hundred forty sisters in the province. Since then, our province joined with Canada (adding a small number of sisters), and our median age has gone up about ten years to eightyish. Our total population has decreased to below two hundred in this province. To my knowledge, there are no more communities of seven, and far fewer communities in general. More sisters live in groups of two or three or in larger groups in independent or assisted living, or even nursing care. In the months after my first vows in 2012, there was at least one sister death per week for thirteen weeks. I might have the numbers wrong because I stopped counting. I just couldn't and wouldn't keep track.

Dwelling on those statistics can really bring me low, not just because they are discouraging but also because they represent sisters that I know and love. Sisters who love me, and who show me how to be a Religious of the Sacred Heart. I certainly didn't know all the sisters who were dying in those weeks, but I knew Claude, who taught me that she never said no when the order asked her to do something, because she had been given so much that she could never repay it in her lifetime. I knew Pat, who had experienced a catastrophic brain injury in the prime of her life, and who taught me that although her life was different now (she knew it), that she was filled with joy and meaningful prayer. I met Claire when she was ninety-nine, studying Spanish from a special chair to hold her crippled body. I knew I met her standards when she gave me a thumbs up as I left the room. A tender conversation with Lil in the months before her death began with her asking me to come to her room to talk—she then asked me if I thought women would ever be ordained. She was ninety-nine and died shortly before her next birthday. From these and from so many sisters I learned what it felt like to be loved and respected just for being me. And I learned to love and respect them for their own uniqueness and beauty.

The Society of the Sacred Heart was founded in 1800 by Madeleine Sophie Barat, in a world that was marked by violence, despair, and profound change, not too unlike our own. France as Sophie experienced was torn by civil war and societal revolution. The very real threat of death faced those who had particular beliefs or birthright. The church was caught in this revolutionary violence. Yet the dominant teachings and spirituality upheld by the Catholic Church kept people discouraged and oppressed, as well. Jansenism, with its influence of Calvinistic thought, emphasized the sinful nature of human beings and the need for them to access God only through the intercession of the priesthood. Sophie had this spirituality ingrained in her from an early age, and eventually she realized that the world needed to know God's love more—a love unconditional and eternal, not bound by human ways or affected by human error. The imagery of the Sacred Heart of Jesus, enshrined in her family home,[1] provided the antidote of love and acceptance to the dis-ease of a condemning God. The Society of the Sacred Heart was thus born from the world's need to be loved and honored, to escape the desolation of Jansenism's negative anthropology.

Sophie's first vision of the Society of the Sacred Heart and the need it met in the world spread quickly from France to the New World and into dozens of countries. At first, the ministry of the Society of the Sacred Heart was limited to education, focusing on the education of girls with the goal of providing order and meaning to all of society through

---

[1] This in itself was taken as an act of defiance against the revolutionary government in France, though there is some indication that Mrs. Barat was not fully aware of this. She enshrined it when it came as a gift from her son, who was a seminarian.

educating its women. Women from the higher levels of society would be educated to shape the minds of their husbands and children, who would then bring this mentality from the home into the public sphere. (Remember that women in the nineteenth century were not expected to lead public lives.) By educating rather wealthy women in boarding schools, financial resources were created that allowed for schools for poor children to learn basic education and skills that could support their families. The system of separate but connected boarding schools and free schools worked well in a hierarchical society where one social class was supposed to be kept separate from another.

The social stratification of France in the nineteenth century did not translate well to the American frontier and beyond. When Sophie's friend and sister, Philippine Duchesne, came to St. Charles, Missouri, and started schools in the Louisiana territory and the American states that would be carved out of it, the system was slowly modified to meet the local needs. At first, the French system was copied, but eventually the separation of social classes fell out of favor in the more egalitarian American culture. The Society of the Sacred Heart then opened academies for girls with wealthier families, orphanages for poor children, and participated in some of the local Catholic schools that were being run by parishes and dioceses. Philippine struggled to adapt to a new culture without guidance from Sophie. Yet she did what was necessary to share the love of God with those around her, which formed the core of her call to life as an RSCJ. She lived the cultural and physical privation of the American frontier, adapted the cloister when it was necessary for the sisters to have greater freedom of movement, and remained the local superior of the American houses even when that form of leadership was seemingly beyond her capacity. Where Sophie's bold clarity of the need to share God's love launched the Society of the Sacred

Heart, Philippine's courageous leadership in the face of scarcity and profound need allowed it to flourish in entirely new circumstances.

Today's rapidly changing world calls for both the bold clarity of Sophie and the courageous leadership of Philippine, together declaring the love of God as present and giving life here and now. This charism addresses:

- The belovedness of each human person.

- The closeness of the Heart of Jesus to each one, especially in a lonely world.

- The beauty of diversity, which illustrates God's great imagination and unites us as the Trinity is one.

- Our own humility in recognizing the infinity of God and the lack of clear answers.

Envisioning these characteristics of my own congregation's charism as tiny elements in the grand project of bringing present God's reign, the need for all charisms to work together becomes more and more apparent. This charism, in fact, leads us to work together as part of a wider shared call to religious life, to a global sisterhood. But first, it is worth dwelling on each of the characteristics listed above, viewing them both as guides for how we treat each other as individuals and as a glimpse of the grand vision God wants for all of us together and on our planet. Then, in these characteristics, we can find ways to be together as part of the global sisterhood as well.

1. Each human person is beloved.

The dignity of the human person is the core of the message we have been given in the Gospels, drawn from the centuries of history shared with us in the Old Testament.

Just as the prophets remind us that God knew us in the womb before we were created, so also Jesus tells us that every hair on our head has been counted by God. We are more precious to God than we can possibly imagine. Jesus is constantly reminding those who are broken and wounded that they are forgiven and loved by God. (Note that he reminds the haughty that they are sinful—those who know that they are sinful need to hear that they are loved.) Recognizing my own belovedness has been a journey supported by the sisters who helped me see how much God loves me—not just "everyone," but *me* personally, with all of my gifts, all of my foibles, all of my woundedness, and all of my blessedness. A recent congregational document reminds us that we are "blessed and broken"—all of us, and the entire world.

The natural (or supernatural?) response to the deep knowledge that God loves *me* is to share that knowledge with others, especially those who most need to hear that message. I don't have to go far to encounter those who need to hear it. How does this affect me? It helps me see past the parts of people that I find unattractive or distracting to see the person in front of me in a genuine and true way. It helps me to be present to them as God has been present to me (in my own tiny non-divine way).

Seeing the world through these eyes also helps us to see the potential present in everything. God's love is extravagant, touching not just the people I meet on a daily basis but even the challenges that exist in the wider world: God loves Donald Trump and Vladimir Putin, Elon Musk and Beyoncé, Pope Francis and Maya Angelou. Belovedness doesn't mean that someone is always right or that bad actions should not have consequences, but it does mean that there is goodness in everyone. Everyone. In a world of social media and seemingly anonymous hate-posting, it's easy to forget that a human being is on the other end of that comment or tweet. And that human being is beloved, just as I am beloved.

2. In a lonely world, the Sacred Heart of Jesus reminds us that God is close by, that we have companions.

"Let the children come to me," Jesus tells his followers. The glory of children is their ability to remain in the present moment. As the "favorite auntie," I can vouch that being with the children means being together, being loved, and most certainly never being alone. Jesus calls to us in the same way—*Come to me, let me be your family, your community, your best friend, your brother*. The Dominican Timothy Radcliffe describes God's love as both deep and personal (like the love between spouses) and broad and all encompassing, which is the love modeled by religious who have vowed to live celibacy. That vow of celibacy brings with it freedom to befriend those who are alone or lonely in a special way. Yes, the spirituality of the Sacred Heart is a reminder that we are not alone; and our ability to place our human selves in the presence of those who are lonely likewise makes present Jesus and his heart.

Religious life brings its own companions, both from among other religious and from among lay people who share in the charism and life. My own experience of religious life began when I moved into the community as a candidate. This happened to be shortly after the earthquake and tsunami that killed thousands of people in Indonesia. I encountered this natural disaster in a new way, because suddenly I knew people, our own sisters, who lived in Indonesia, and we had word from them about the impact of the tsunami on the people of Indonesia. A similar situation occurred when the Fukushima disaster happened in Japan: shortly afterward, a Japanese sister was visiting our community and we were able to ask her personally about what had happened, how our sisters were, and whose families were affected. When these sisters tell their stories, it's not just about them as individuals; we also learn of the communal heartache and trauma that the country as a whole experiences. We are never alone, and our companions genuinely care for one another.

3. There is beauty in diversity, which leads to greater wholeness and unity.

In Sacred Heart education, each human being's unique gifts and calling must be honored and encouraged to grow according to God's call for her. Sophie developed close personal relationships with individual sisters, whom she guided and advised according to their individual needs. My own experience of formation in the Society reflected this recognition of the uniqueness of each one, the value we place on our differences, and the attempt to meet each one's unique needs. It is often said that when a new member is welcomed into a community, it's not just about recognizing how that individual will fit into the community; it is also a decision to allow the whole community to be changed by that person's presence. We can only be complete when all are welcomed and honored.

We know that our world has different needs that are met by the different gifts people bring, and that the diversity we bring together leads to greater wholeness. St. Paul uses that great image of "one body and many parts"—without each unique organ or limb, we are missing something essential. If we really believe that each human being is created in the image and likeness of God, then what does our diversity tell us about who God is? And how can we begin to appreciate God's fullness if we can't appreciate and admire God's likeness in one another?

Beyond appreciation for the diversity of our world, we need to honor and cherish the differences that bring us together. God's own self gives us the example of unity-with-diversity, as the Trinity, three distinct Persons bound together with the power of Love. Over the last several years we have seen an outcry against discrimination alongside overtly hateful and racist speech and actions. We have watched as nations literally built walls to keep "them" away from us. We build our own walls on social media and in neighborhoods where we only encounter people who look, act, and think in ways that are similar to ourselves.

Honoring and celebrating our differences is another way to understand who God is, in a more complete way than we can if the only "image of God" we see is in people who look like us. Yet, even in most of our congregations, we struggle with the reality of diversity. Most Catholic sisters in the United States are older women of European descent, whose lives in community have developed patterns in which they feel comfortable. Honoring and celebrating diversity requires changing patterns of life and thought so that each one can express herself fully and be equally at home in the community's life. Our charisms call us to greater openness to witness to the fullness of the image and likeness of God in our world.

4. We live with ambiguity, in the humble knowledge that God holds all of us in safety.

"God can do infinitely more than we can ask or imagine" (Eph 3:20). When I was discerning my way into the community, the vocation director used this phrase over and over again in prayer and written notes to me. It resonated with me then and continues to speak to the mystery of God that draws me closer and closer. I often marvel as a theologian that I will never exhaust the subject matter because God is infinite! There is always more to learn and explore, and as someone who enjoys that process, it brings me great joy and consolation.

Not knowing is also a humbling feeling. My capacity is limited. Not only that, but black and white answers are not the norm—we live in shades of uncertainty and ignorance. My congregation was founded during the French Revolution, at a time and place where the political and social world changed from day to day. Religious orders were tolerated one day and under threat of expulsion or death the next. Sophie could not imagine all the challenges she would encounter in preserving the foundation of the Society. And then, Philippine Duchesne took a group of sisters to live in the wilderness of North America, where they encountered a completely different situation. They wrote home in astonishment at the things they saw.

Our world today teaches us that we can figure things out with certainty through scientific exploration, and we can find answers to any questions we have by asking Alexa or Siri. There is a lot of good in having ready access to information. If it brings the expectation that we have answers for everything, then we have lost sight of our reliance on God and on others. We must resist the impulse to consider our own human minds superior to the mystery that permeates our world.

What happens when we remember that we are not God? When we remember that our human capacity for reason and thought—while brilliant—cannot answer every human problem with certainty? When we remember that we started all the problems in the world that we are now trying to solve? As we consider the future of religious life, we must remember that we don't have the answers, and we don't know what God has in store for us.

What we can do is trust. We don't need to know the answers, because God is holding us close and will take care of us. We are precious to God, each one of us in all of our diversity. And God's imagination is infinite—we do not know and can't imagine what will happen, but we can trust that God's love and compassion will be with us no matter what.

These four characteristics of the charism of the Society of the Sacred Heart are by no means the only marks of that charism, and they are definitely shared with other orders— and I would even say all Christians. These qualities point to the necessity of a global sisterhood. They call us to think bigger than ourselves, than one congregation, than one small group, in order to imagine more fully the diversity and expansiveness of God. So, how do these four qualities— the belovedness of each human person, the closeness of Jesus to all of us, the beauty of diversity and its union in the love of God, and the humility of humanity in light of the infinity of God—how do they draw us toward a global sisterhood?

We believe that God created each of us in God's own image. Religious orders, too, express God's likeness by working toward the kingdom of God in one little corner of the world. Just as the beauty of each of God's creations gives us a glimpse of God's fullness, so too the work and spirit of each congregation gives us a glimpse of the fullness of the kingdom. We need the religious who feed the poor, those who focus on healthcare, those who focus on care for creation, those who advocate for change in policies, those who educate, and on and on. Any one congregation cannot do it all. And at the same time, we need the spiritual language of each one—the Society of the Sacred Heart's language around Jesus' Heart, the Dominicans' talk of truth, the Congregation of St. Joseph's focus on dear neighbor, the Jesuits' focus on the glory of God, the Franciscans' "Peace and All Good." When we put them all together, the works and spirit of the different congregations create a prism by which we can see all the different facets of God's self and the works of God's kingdom. We need one another.

Jesus is close to each one, to each individual and to each group. We often hear language of "diminishment" and fear that we are not going to be there for the future, that one or another congregation has completed their mission here on earth. Grief is a lonely road, but it is not walked alone. Jesus doesn't want us to walk it alone, and companions are ready to accompany us at every stage. One of my first experiences of religious life was a meeting of Giving Voice, a group for women religious under fifty. In that group of sisters from all congregations, I found companions in formation and in my age cohort, neither of which existed in my own province. Collaboration and accompanying one another is already a definitive characteristic of religious life. Formation programs have been intercongregational for generations of sisters, leadership teams have relied on one another for support and expertise, and even some apostolates bring together sisters of different congregations to collaborate. We have companions, and we are not alone on our unique paths. We need one another.

The diverse members of a single congregation come together as one—and the diverse congregations that we each represent are also called to unite. Together we represent more clearly the unity of God, a mirror hazily showing the Trinity. I have heard the fear expressed that if we do come together in one global sisterhood, we would lose each congregation's uniqueness. Just as we are called to honor human diversity without pretending that we are all the same, so too for congregations we must honor the differences and allow them to further God's vision in their unique ways. When I meet with friends from different congregations, I find that it strengthens my call to be an RSCJ because understanding the charisms of other orders highlights the reasons I feel strongly called to my own. I'm also able to better speak about my own charism because we often share about who we are and how we are called. Instead of pulling me away from my congregation, sharing with others strengthens my sense of belonging to it. We need one another.

Finally, we are called to humility and to trusting in God's tender care. St. Madeleine Sophie frequently cited Jesus' words: "Learn from me, for I am meek and humble of heart" (Matt 11:29). Humility in God is most profoundly represented in the Incarnation: God became human, giving up omnipotence, omniscience, infinity, in order to become completely dependent on a human mother—on humanity, on *us*. Imagine if we could give up our status, our security, our retirement accounts, so that we could rely entirely on God's providence for all that we need. More realistically, what if we recognized that even with all the safeguards we have put in place, we still can't do it ourselves, that we rely completely on God? Would that, then, encourage our partnerships with other congregations, to learn from them and share our abundance of gifts? In humility, let's remember that no one person or group has all the answers, and that with each other we can find support for what we lack and a bigger image of the whole that God offers us. We need one another.

The beauty of religious life today is that there is something for everyone: while I felt the call to share God's love with others, each sister in this book would describe her call using different language. Regardless of the call, it is about bringing God into the world in my own way, which draws upon the tradition of sisters I follow as an RSCJ. In this, I am bound not just to my sisters, but to the global sisterhood, each of us giving ourselves to God and the world. All of us from all congregations working together will still find plenty of need, plenty of people who long for God's love and presence in their lives. Our different expressions of that gift highlight the breadth of God's presence.

8

Reseeding, Sprouting, and Rooting Deeply

Monica Marie Cardona, VDMF

In contrast to the other chapters of this book, I share from the context of a relatively new institute of consecrated life, which the Dicastery for Institutes of Consecrated Life and Societies of Apostolic Life is now calling an "Ecclesial Family of Consecrated Life," because three different branches which share the same charism, spirituality, and mission are united under one governing structure. The Verbum Dei Missionary Fraternity, founded by Reverend Jaime Bonet in 1963, reignited the same charism that many other religious groups have lived throughout the centuries: the call of the first apostles to proclaim the kerygma, the transforming message of the Resurrected Christ who invites us to continual transformation and conversion through our contemplative relationship with the Word of God. Born in Spain and spreading rather quickly throughout the world into thirty-three countries, part of our community's missionary reality is its international dimension. In addition, we are not only a female institute of consecrated life, but the fraternity includes two other branches: the male branch, composed of priests and brothers, and the married couples' branch. This diversity is a complementary, precious, and challenging mix. In this chapter, I would like to share about Verbum Dei as one of the new seeds that has sprouted after Vatican II. This may give us a clue as to where the church is headed, what is essential in our life of consecration, and why it is vital to remain firmly rooted.

We are merely sixty-one years old, so we are still figuring things out. Despite this short history, only recently coming out of our foundational period and still transitioning in the current stage of institutionalization, we too have not been immune to the crisis which is affecting most of religious and consecrated life in recent years. Our median age is much lower than most other religious communities and we do not possess as many structures or properties, but we have also been affected by fewer vocations, recent exits from the middle-life age range, and increasing concern for a greater economic stability after our founding years of great charismatic enthusiasm and little to no thought about the long-term future. We all agree the time has come to tackle these issues and redefine the meaning of what perhaps originally had another significance: providence, full-time apostolic and missionary dedication, and radicality in our consecration, amongst other questions.

We have lived intensely and are in the process of over-coming the initial founding years of fervor and enthusiasm by undergoing the necessary purification and confrontation with reality. The purification consists in humbly recognizing that we do not possess the "only" or "best" way to live a consecrated missionary life. We are just one of many precious charisms in the church, and we have a treasure to offer in continuity with the rich spirituality that has been expressed and lived over the centuries.

What is our specific contribution to the church? Each religious family has a specialization to share with the church. The Jesuits offer a specific method of discernment and the Ignatian Spiritual Exercises, the Salesians contribute their dynamic work with youth, the Benedictines give their hospitality and contemplative focus of *ora et labora*, while the Franciscans provide a specific witness and solidarity with the poor. Each charism enriches the totality of the Body of Christ and contributes its unique specialization in order to heal Christ. The focus of Verbum Dei is the Word of God and our numerous ways of bringing people to an intimate encounter with Christ through the Word by helping them cultivate a living relationship with this Word made flesh. Our missionary platforms vary creatively from one corner of the world to the next and across the diverse cultures with which we have had the privilege of working. At center stage has been the importance of our contemplative prayer with the Word, as well as our living and existential "preaching" and sharing of this Word. In the same way the first apostles experienced their missionary passion, we have touched a love and joy so deep that, "We cannot stop speaking of what we have seen and heard" (Acts 4:20).

Past, Present, and Looking Forward

These past years I have had the opportunity to serve my community as a councilor on the female branch council and on the general board. This historical time and the epochal change we are witnessing has been particularly challenging due to the worldwide pandemic, which has brought all of us to a halt and made us reconsider our options and commitments. It has forced us to reframe what we find worthwhile in our lives. We have perceived that it has also served to awaken an unease in many of our members around different issues that we need to resolve from our past and present. This experience of touching many realities of my community from the perspective of the service in the government has been unique and very illuminating.

One lesson that is becoming apparent is the need to value and be grateful for the road traveled thus far. Undoubtedly there have been many failures and mistakes, but to recognize, acknowledge, and give thanks for the positive and beautiful moments of our history is essential. To tell our stories and listen to each other's is a way of celebrating and showing gratitude for our roots. These roots are those which allow our community to be standing at present. Our human tendency is to look back from the point of view of our wounds, our deceptions, and our disappointments, and if we do not tackle and heal the wounds from our past, they color the entire reading of our history—this is unfortunate, because there is so much more that is actually gift and grace.

Rootedness gives stability in the midst of a quickly changing world that only seems to become more unstable as time passes. For this reason, regardless of the ups and downs of our history, we must cultivate a deep gratitude for our roots. To be "radical" means to be connected to our roots and living from what is essential. This permits us to have a strong sense of belonging and therefore assume responsibility from our place within the entire structure. We cannot sit by complacently waiting for someone else to do what needs to be done. Synodality is a call to be coresponsible and ask questions such as: How can we build from this point onward? How can we look forward without allowing our past frustrations to weigh us down or hold us back? Learning to look back with gratitude and humility and to look forward with sharp eyes of creative projection is vital for the growth of the community and its connectedness with its roots.

Roots, Rocks, and Foundations

When I studied church history many years ago, one of the things that most caught my attention was that after the first centuries of Christian persecution when the church was established and approved by the Roman Empire, the Desert Mothers and Fathers actively sought to live the radicality of their Christian life and faith with a deeper fervor and asceticism. These were the very roots of consecrated life as we know it today. This ascetic life was their way of giving "witness" to God's love, and it is the same root of the Greek word which means martyr. In fact, these beginnings of consecrated life were also referred to as "white martyrdom." What does it mean to be a martyr today? How can we best witness our faith, so as to provoke questions in those who see us? How can consecrated life today be a sign of eternal life? What needs renewal in our lives and communities to reawaken this desire for a radical following of Christ?

When a living organism is in crisis, it may often help it to survive and thrive if it goes to its roots. The only way we can overcome the challenges and difficulties inherent to our particular countercultural vocation of witnessing to Christ's love is when we deeply root and ground ourselves in Christ and when we experience the strong call to identification and communion with Christ. Without this base and foundation, everything else will eventually fall apart.

Speaking of roots, I love to observe and learn the fascinating lessons that nature teaches us, and which can speak deeply to our hearts. Trees that grow on rocky cliffs, the seemingly worst imaginable growing conditions, dry and exposed to the elements, offer us a profound lesson. One might not expect these trees growing on rocks to live for very long, but "paradoxically when trees do grow in these tough cliff environments, they can actually outlive their counterparts in a rich forest environment by a factor of 20 or more."[1] Trees in these harsh environments reap benefits because they face less competition from other plants. "Trees on cliffs will often stay small, which lessens the need for nutrients and protects them from becoming weak and blowing over."[2]

Several details touch me about the growth of trees on rocky cliffs. First, this historical moment in the world and in the church is filled with the harshness of unpredictability. From the climate crisis to a society swept up by the bombardment of social media, recovering from a global pandemic, struck by war and the continuous movements of peoples, no one can be indifferent to a series of changes and challenges that threaten to uproot the most firmly rooted person. These rocky cliffs are the times we live in. The lesson is to grow roots that reach deeper than the risks and threats, in order to find nourishment where it lies. Only when one is rooted can one withstand the storm. Nothing else is capable of anchoring us quite in the same way as God can. There is not much to compete with the nourishment that we drink from God, any other source proves to be temporal and minimal. Interestingly a factor for survival is "staying small." This reminds us of the Gospel where Jesus invites us to be like little children (Luke 18:16 and Mark 10:15). A fundamental aspect of our call to follow Christ is humility. This is not to say we cannot do great things as Jesus has promised, but that we must never lose touch with our essence as God's limited creatures.

---

[1] Scout Wilkins, "How Trees Grow in Rocks," May 19, 2018, accessed March 13, 2024, https://travelinglight.life/how-trees-grow-in-rocks/.

[2] Wilkins, "How Trees Grow in Rocks."

The Rock of Contemplation

The image of rocky cliffs cannot but remind me of several pilgrimage sites that I have visited in recent years. The caves of Sts. Benedict and Scholastica in Subiaco, the caves of Francis and his companions in Assisi, the cave of Ignatius of Loyola in Manresa, looking toward the mountains of Montserrat where there are still more caves—these are just a few. Great saints and mystics often retreated away into the caves seeking their solitude and silence in order to truly listen to God. Great mystical experiences come from climbing mountains and scaling rocks, experiencing the challenge of the ascent and the cool refreshing shade of a rocky mountain under the scorching sun. "See there is a place by me where you shall stand on the rock. And while my glory passes by, I will put you in a cleft of the rock." This is what God told Moses in Exodus 33:21-23, where God would reveal himself. A hole in the rock, in other words, a cave which is a symbol of the deepest encounter with oneself and with God. One must remain, one must learn to be stable and allow it to become rooted and part of one's life, especially when there is so much change and instability.

Coming back to that tree rooted in the rocky clefts of the mountain and thriving against all odds, its roots have needed to grow longer. Those roots grow through the experience of contemplation. What a challenging call in the midst of a world full of impact, noise, change and yet what tremendous power we draw from our rootedness in prayer and contemplation. If consecrated life is not rooted in a deep life of contemplative prayer, it will not survive. We can do many good works, work side by side with the poorest of the poor, serve in many important ways, be highly educated and significant on intellectual and academic levels, have leadership roles of great power and influence, but if our roots are not firm in our personal and mystical relationship with God, we will not survive the winds of discouragement, the harsh reality of injustice, and the crude storms of deception.

The New Shoots of Verbum Dei: Contemplation, Synodality, and Ecclesiality

The intuition of our founder, Jaime Bonet, has marked in the Verbum Dei Missionary Fraternity a return to a deeply contemplative life amid our missionary action. Without ever acquiring a monastic piety, style, or rhythm of prayer, the personal encounter with Christ and the time we dedicate to it has been primordial in our way of life from the very beginnings of Verbum Dei. We are accustomed to long periods of silent prayer and contemplation with the Word of God and every year we set aside the time for a month of spiritual exercises in complete silence based on the Word of God. Sometimes this option is not easy to understand, nor has it been easy to defend, but these means have accompanied us from our foundation, and these intuitions cannot be overlooked or forgotten if we are to live faithfully our specific charism and spirituality. These are the roots of our calling and mission to go into the world and share the Good News in new and creative ways. Without a deeply contemplative life, what hope can we preach to the brokenhearted, what faith can we offer to the desolate, and what love can we give to those in need?

Being very much "in fashion" with the present-day calling of the church to live and practice synodality, our institute boasts of having three branches, which we refer to as our "ecclesiality." Women, lay married couples, priests, and brothers all sit at the same round table. It is complex, and in many moments very challenging, but it is also a very beautiful experience that calls us to a constant conversion. It would be easier and faster to go our own separate ways, but this witness of life of walking together can also be understood as part of our mission. In today's church it seems to be the grand innovation. However, numerous founders in years past had dreamed of keeping their male and female institutes united, but either it was not permitted or simply not yet the right time. Today, the time has come and this communion among the branches is undoubtedly a sign of collaboration and co-responsibility pointing toward the kingdom. There is still so much work to be done, we are not there yet, but the journey is fascinating.

Another specific innovation of our ecclesial family is the way we form and empower the lay. The call of our charism to make disciples and form apostles, who in turn form others, invites us to live a constant dynamic of the continuation of our missionary work. This not only permits a certain itinerancy to some extent, allowing us to move and spread to other places, but it continues the movement of handing over the baton of leadership. This is a prime example of what it means that the Word of God and the mission of the church is for all and not only for ordained ministers. The Second Vatican Council inaugurated this change, giving great responsibility to the people of God, particularly women and the laity. In many ways I see that the future of our ministries, apostolates, and communities lies in the sense of ownership and responsibility that the laity take on. The survival and growth of our missionary calling and charismatic identity depends on how much we share our leadership with the laity and hand over responsibilities to them. After all, the church is primarily the people of God, not just those fully dedicated, such as the hierarchy or the consecrated, and we are still walking toward the transformation of our understanding of church.

The specific contribution of our consecrated witness is like the yeast in the dough. It is not always glamourous, nor does it necessarily shine brightly in obvious ways, yet our life is a light set on a lampstand and a point of reference for the Verbum Dei family and the church. As modern post-conciliar missionaries who have never worn habits, we blend in with, and in some ways can't be told apart from, the people of God. This is beautiful because what is essential is invisible to the eye. Yet there is something deeper that is noticed even if we do not make an effort. The witness of life, the unpresumptuous simplicity, and gentle leadership cannot be mistaken, and our aim is to serve and form the Verbum Dei missionary disciples by example, as Jesus who washed the feet of his disciples. We can only continue to dream and hope that young women and men may feel the attraction and desire to live and witness these new expressions of consecrated life for today's world.

9

Reseeding Religious Life from the Lens of Integral Living

Nkechi Iwuoha, PHJC

Reseeding religious life furthers the conversation on the prophetic call of religious women and men to integral living as we engage the charisms of the founders/foundresses of our various congregations. It is a call to holistic living as echoed in the call of Pope Francis in *Laudato Si'*, which invites us to a way of being and ministry that is modeled on the concept of integral ecology. For centuries, religious life has been largely lived from the viewpoint of a fragmented vocation, where we lived and carried out our ministries in silos. The old order saw the evangelical counsels in isolation from a holistic sense of mission. With this understanding, religious life was compartmentalized and devoid of integral thinking. This concept of religious life was also exported by the missionaries to missions and various cultures across the globe. It is imperative to note that this is what all these missionaries knew and learned from their formators when they were sent on mission. Hence, in reseeding religious life, I invite us to explore this life lived in communion and total abandonment from the following perspectives: social, economic, political, cultural, and spiritual reseeding of religious life, each of which captures holistic living as a challenge to vowed life.

Social Ecology

Religious life as a call to live the Gospel signifies the symbol of social ecology. The value of the Gospel then becomes a driving force for relating to others with respect, inclusion, and compassion. When we speak of the social nature of reseeding religious life, we are talking about the social relationships of belonging, inclusion, mutuality, and solidarity. This embraces every social unit, from the primary social group, the family, to wider local, national, and international communities and institutions. In my community, the Poor Handmaids of Jesus Christ, we embrace, as one of our charisms, attentiveness to interdependence in meeting the needs of the vulnerable as we recognize the collective wisdom of individual communities and persons to engage in shared ministry to homeless women and children in Gary, Indiana. This engagement speaks to the concept of inclusion and solidarity with marginalized groups. As numbers of religious men and women decrease in the Northern Hemisphere, we are called to authentically live the vows. The walls of assuming status and of feeling set apart have crumbled, and we are left to speak with our lives and bear witness to the risen Lord. We are challenged as vowed members to think integrally and outside the boundaries of individual congregations and charisms, to thinking globally and acting locally, seeing our lives from the context of the charism of religious life that binds the Southern and Northern Hemispheres in bonds of sister/brotherhood. Is this then not what Jesus prayed for? "That they may be one as you and I are one: that the world may believe that you have sent me" (John 17:21-23).

Economic Ecology

Reseeding religious life challenges and invites us to a frugal lifestyle, like Mary Mother of God, and a life modeled by our founding mothers and fathers to serve and break open the root causes of poverty that are anchored in addressing systems that hold the poor and marginalized hostage. When we speak of the economic nature of integral ecology, and the challenge to vowed people, we envision an economic sphere that serves the rightful needs of all individuals and all societies, rather than economies that exploit and perpetuate the artificial needs of consumeristic societies. This requires that the economy respect the finite limits of the natural world. It is also an invitation to be the voice helping the people we serve to recognize their rights in a society laden with oppression. This call is more urgent for reseeding life in the Southern Hemisphere. For instance, where I come from in Nigeria, religious life is still being lived from the old model of filling convents with women and formation programs that are not broad enough to raise the pertinent questions that confront society, but rather are largely based on offering direct service to the people. We run health centers, social centers, and schools. My experience of being a Nigerian sister pioneer, helping to found the Poor Handmaid community in Nigeria, opened my eyes to ask the questions: What should we be doing as we face a future that could be a time of decreased vocations? How can we engage in an educational process for younger religious that departs from entitlement, maintaining the status quo, and attachment to individual charisms and instead focuses on a collective, collaborative, and simpler engagement with God's people? This scenario of filling convents is no longer a reality in the United States and Europe, but formation continues to be done in isolation—until now, congregations worked alone and were in some cases in competition with each other.

For these reasons, reseeding religious life should be an ongoing process that embodies the God who continues to call men and women who will be able to adapt themselves to the changing times, which call us to global sisterhood in addressing systems that chain those we serve. It is an invitation for women religious who are fearless, courageous, selfless, committed, dialogical, and prayerfully listening to the promptings of the Spirit to embrace the struggle for justice. It is a call to be prophets who are open and able to evaluate and critically analyze the impact of national and international politics, policies and laws that are promulgated in our various lands and on the people we serve. It is a call to be attuned to global news with objectivity and to cultivate the ability to understand the obstacles militating against our efforts to announce the reign of God. In the absence of this awareness, then, religious men and women would be like the child who came to school but fell asleep. When the teacher asked, "Junior, what is the answer to the question I just asked?" Junior replied, "Sorry teacher, in the first place, I did not hear the question."

A Call to Engage Political Ecology

Religious women have for many centuries been involved in the care of human suffering through education, healthcare, and social work. In this way, they respond to the call of the Father to go to the ends of the earth proclaiming the Good News. They have desired and have given equitable attention to the sick and injured in various parts of the world, in this way providing them with equal access to basic healthcare.

When we speak of the political nature of integral ecology and engagement of religious women, we are referring to the policies and practices that shape and govern society and demand equitable access and justice for all, healthcare being a prime example. Reseeding religious life then calls for a critical analysis of how political systems impact the people of God we serve, thus depriving them of basic needs and taking away their dignity. One of the charisms of the Poor Handmaids is attentiveness to the marginalized and vulnerable. We, as an international community, continue to challenge ourselves to be protective of this population and to face our own prejudices by realizing our potential to evolve our thinking to go beyond problem-solving and direct services to stimulate and become a catalyst for systemic change. We are also mindful that living with "enoughness" means abundance for all. This reinforces our vow of poverty, that others may live and have life to the fullest by standing with the poor and the powerless. The prophets of today also need to interrupt the status quo by unmasking and deconstructing the structures of our time. The regular Sunday liturgy needs also to be seen as an opportunity for the gathering of the faith community to be nurtured and revitalized for prophetic action in and for the world, as our lives continue to be acts of worship.

Cultural Ecology

Reseeding religious life is an invitation to live radical welcome as Christ did in his time with all who are on the margins. Religious are reinvited to a down-to-earth emulation of peasant women who mingled with some creativity and resourcefulness in resolving difficult situations. When there is attention on the reseeding of religious life through the lens of cultural ecology, we are presented with an invitation to speak of the respect and appreciation for the rich diversity of cultural/ethnic heritages and ways of life that are intrinsic to who we are as a people. From my experience of living and working in different cultures as a Poor Hand-maid, I have come to realize the advice of St. Paul to the Galatians: "There can be neither Jew nor Greek, there can be neither slave nor free person, there can be neither male nor female—for we are all one in Christ Jesus" (Gal 3:28-29). In community, I have felt the tensions created by isms: racism, tribalism, clannism, ageism, and sexism. I have directly or indirectly been impacted by these levels of discrimination. It became apparent to me that community is not just being physically under one roof, playing games, partying, and watching television together. Rather, reseeding religious life must emphasize the challenge to go beyond the outward expression of community building. True reseeding occurs when we realize that we are called to carry each other, support each other, and be in solidarity with one another. It is a call to embrace one another within and across community in a way that lets go of fear to embrace diversity, equity, and inclusion, not only for the people we are missioned to serve, but also to the individual sisters. It also calls us to look inward to our own brokenness, as we navigate ways to address unjust structures of racism, bias, and prejudice that sit and dwell within convent walls. To me, living mission from this lens affirms the evangelical counsel of chastity as a call of God to a radical love, welcome, and acceptance of all God's creation and cultures. My community is gradually growing into an awareness of such isms and finding tools to enhance our capacity and desire for intentionality in speaking about our internationality and naming our flaws in growing toward interculturality. It then becomes imperative to be patient with and embrace each culture as holy without imposing our ways of doing things, but acknowledging the evolutionary stages of our lives together. Hence it becomes necessary to internalize the art of cultural competence as we adhere to advice attributed to a mystic philosopher of ancient China, Laozi: "Go to the people. Live with them. Learn from them. Love them. Start with what they know. Build with what they have. But with the best leaders, when the work is done, the task accomplished, the people will say 'We have done this ourselves.'"

A Heart as a Symbol of Spiritual Ecology

In reseeding religious life, we are then asked to embrace the ways of God, seeing again with our heart the compassion, mercy, and love that God intends for our relationship with all of creation. When we speak of the spiritual nature of integral ecology, we are recognizing that at the heart of the ecological crisis lies a deep human and spiritual crisis, in that we have forgotten who we are and where we have come from. This calls for an ecological conversion. It is a call to be aware of who we vowed to be: spiritual women seeking God through one another. We are called to life in communion (interpersonal relationship), and thus as prophets we need to perfect the art of relationship. The ability to navigate interpersonal relationships will help men and women both in initial and ongoing formation to master ways to relate to God's people on the missions. This conversion of heart deepens our understanding of integral living as not just a journey of personal growth, but a collective journey of evolutionary deepening, an essential spiritual journey that speaks to the salvation of the world, both planet and people, in and through the cosmic Christ. My conviction is that in this reseeding process, religious are first missioned to self and to each other, and then we can gain better skills to give what we possess. Jesus washes the feet of his disciples, inspiring humanity to take up the basin and the towel. Through this gesture, God calls us into deeper and greater communion with Godself. Day after day we are invited to take up the basin and the towel. The tenderness of the towel and the willingness of the water inspire us. The call is to community, the impoverished power that sets the soul free and the humility to take the basin and the towel.

In reseeding religious life, we gain an understanding that tending the wounds of the poor and the planet becomes an awakening, calling us to embrace the intersection of the various ecologies: social, economic, environmental, political, cultural, and spiritual. In living into this intersection, we will continue to realize that our founders and foundresses invite us to fill our lives and our bags full of these ecologies, impacting one another by the very fact of their integral nature. We will then be challenged to ask ourselves as individuals and as a community how we are tending to the cries of the poor and the cries of the planet in our day through an integral lens of living the evangelical counsels. We are then encouraged to explore the question: What is our individual congregational charism and spirituality revealing to us as we face the future of reseeding religious life to harness a harvest of holistic thinking and live into the emerging future of religious life? Because reseeding religious life calls for a prophetic radical stance, those who want to embark on this journey should be asking themselves questions such as Joan Chittister asked: What do great prophets such as Amos, Hosea, Isaiah, Micah, Ezekiel, and Jesus have in common with the religious? As she answers: All of them were simple souls like you and me. All of them loved without limit, burned with an enduring patience, were afire with God, and proclaimed a new vision.

The dreaming of this new vision must continue to expand, to include newer and younger members from diverse cultures, and to engage in a contemplative dialogue on the emerging future of religious life. We must reflect on the call of synodality by listening, being prayerful, engaging in discernment processes, and trusting the Spirit that resides within each of us and among all of us. In this way, we will further interconnection, integration, and interrelationship, which are at the heart of challenging all communities to stay at the table of the conversation on reseeding religious life.

Afterword:
Anticipating the Future

Teresa Maya, CCVI

I cannot wait for the future to find us. I have always longed to see the future, so much so that a provincial once accused me of unnecessary "futuring." More than twenty years ago, I had unsuccessfully tried to explain to our province that "in the future, everyone was going to use the internet to look up things." I was frustrated, especially when I explained that the yellow pages would disappear and the sisters thought I was exaggerating. The provincial team eventually approved our first website more out of sympathy for me than conviction. Rebuked by the whole province, I went about the task of the present with diligence and dedication. I knew then that receding would be a lot of work and that it would be met with a lot of resistance and denial, so I rolled up my sleeves and worked hard with lay people in our ministries to prepare for when sisters would be gone from day-to-day operations. A wise Christian Brother, Salvador Valle, trying to console me, explained that if I was worried about the future, I should prepare the people so that they would be ready when the future came. As a result, I developed formation programs of all kinds, explored the first learning management systems (LMS), and created leadership development retreats and seminars. I was earnest, despite my peers in community who thought I was both being catastrophic and too appreciative of lay collaborators in ministries. At one point, one of them accused me of loving the laity more than our sisters!

Once I was serving in congregational leadership again, I took to the thankless task of organizing finances, accounting structures, updating systems, reviewing property and preparing for elder care when sisters' income could not support everyone. Again, resistance, denial, and fear would keep chipping away at my zeal, but I pushed on, wanting to get all of us to the future. Then, I failed. The pandemic punched the air out of all the strategic plans, and the grief caught up with me. While we had some readiness, the future came suddenly, one funeral at a time, with every wise elder moving to the next level of care. The receding now gathered tsunamic strength and was about to engulf all of us. My term ended, full receding now on the horizon.

Sister Susan Francois, CSJP, and Sister Juliet Mousseau, RSCJ, offer possibilities with this collaborative work to those at a juncture like mine, perhaps overwhelmed by the receding work or exhausted from doing it. They explain that receding has a place, provided it tills the soil of religious life to make it more fertile for the "reseeding" God's abundance is already dispersing around us. They refocus the receding work with purpose—with a *why*—and in so doing, they offer us a future that will require the rest of us to go about reseeding. Susan frames it beautifully: "We are called to risk the bigness of smallness and reseed the next chapter of God's dream for religious life, already present among us." Juliet offers that the reason for this risk is nothing less than God's mission for us, that our congregational charisms are all "tiny elements in the grand project of God's reign." In Juliet's words, the authors challenge us to a charismatic synodality: "Think bigger than ourselves, than one congregation, than one small group, in order to imagine more fully the diversity and expansiveness of God." Receding to reseed is about our faithfulness to God!

The first step to moving forward with their vision is to ask ourselves if we are willing to heed the invitation to recede to reseed. The authors challenge us to stand strong before the waves recede. They point to the other part of the future that is also here, the part that we often miss because we are so busy in this great "inhaling" of the spirit most of our communities are in. They name the parts of the future I have longed to see all this time. They come from the peripheries of community—newer members, international members, those new in leadership—where the seeds of the future sprout first. They challenge us to notice the seeds and the sprouts and to go about reseeding with the same energy and resourcefulness as the receding. Their insight offers hope about the future of religious life in our church, no matter what part of the journey our institutes or our sisters are on. They are already living in this future, and they offer us a bridge into the new that is emerging. Our task is now to cross. Like the poem by Argentinian poet and children's book writer Elsa Isabel Bornermann, the writers have drawn many bridges; it is up to us to cross; no one can do for us.

> I draw bridges
> so you can find me
> A bridge of cloth,
> with my watercolors . . .
> A hanging bridge,
> with brilliant chalk . . .
> Wooden bridges,
> with wooden pencil . . .
> Drawbridges,
> silver, copper . . .

> Indestructible bridges,
> of stone, invisible . . .
> And you . . . Who would think!
> You don't even see them!
> I draw one hundred, ten, one . . .
> You do not cross any of them!
> Yet . . . because I love you . . .
> I draw and wait.
> Beautiful, beautiful bridges
> so you might find me![1]

I want to reflect on a few reasons to heed the invitation to cross to the other side.

In many ways the authors challenge us to a charismatic synodality. Reading their insights invites us to move beyond the stories of our individual religious institutes into the unfolding narrative of all our interconnections. Sister Nkechi Iwuoha, PHJC, explains that we are called to an ecological conversion to understand the connections. They call us to lean into the inter-charismatic spiritual conversations that will energize our distinct charisms and inspire the unfolding of emerging global sisterhood. Each of the authors came of age in a religious life fully engaged in receding but also fully invested in the intercongregational formation efforts, like formation programs or organizations such as Giving Voice. The reflections in this book are a harvest of this intercongregational crop. They can speak from the lived experience of a "more porous, light sharing, global sisterhood," in the words of Sister Tracey Horan, SP, "a sisterhood not limited to the structures of our congregation." The synodal

---

[1] Elsa Isabel Bornemann, "Puentes," in *El libro de los chicos enamorados* (Buenos Aires: Fausto, 1987). Translated by the author.

weaving happens in every chapter; they share encounters and transformations about deepening and broadening their charismatic identity with each conversation.

The honesty with which the sisters address some of the difficult questions facing religious life offers a pathway for the synodal journey ahead. They challenge us to see beyond the parochial and very local tasks of "receding" to discern the patterns emerging in our global sisterhood. We might say they are challenging us to "laudatosificate" our discernment, to see how everything is connected: the new movements of human migration and the evolution of religious life, the need for a church transformed out of its clericalism, the collaboration across charismatic boundaries, and the personal conversion needed to discern honestly. Perhaps we could say that the authors are migrants, some international, some domestic, some generational, all from one way of life into consecrated life. Their migrant experience allows them to voice what they see emerging from the margins of religious life. Sister Chioma Ahanihu, SLW, Sister Katty Huanuco, CCVI, and Sister Monica Marie Cardona, VDMF, name the blessings reseeding in different soil offers. They offer insights from their personal experience about the internationalization of religious institutes in the United States. Without shying from the pain of the racism or discrimination they experienced, they offer a glimpse of the grace welcoming our migrant sisters will mean. After all, we should all feel at home in our respective religious community; we all need a place to call home, as Katty Huanuco gracefully reminds us.

Religious life today toils arduously in the hard, dry ground of "receding," as Houston Incarnate Word Sister Ricca Dimalibot's honest and soul-disturbing words describe. She opens by pondering a question every sister needs to ask herself: "Why do I stay?" She explains that we all tell and retell the story of "why we came," but why we are still here requires honest discernment. When Ricca speaks of the "yoke of leadership," she does so with refreshing transparency. She describes receding work as all-consuming for leaders often unequipped to deal with critical organizational issues. Ricca asks soul-searching questions about this difficult work. She speaks of the administrative, financial, and healthcare tasks we are all longing to have someone else do! Ricca invites us into her journey, enticing our reflection. What is my relationship to this receding task? Have I contributed my part in my institute or do I keep avoiding both the questions and responsibilities? Ricca explains that all of it is done in the "name of serving the greater good." She reminds us that the space between receding and reseeding is not a comfortable one; it is a place of *dis-ease*. How many of us are willing to sacrifice our time, energy, and preferred ministry in the receding work that makes reseeding possible?

The synodal journey for religious life requires resolving its occasionally uncomfortable relationship with the institutional church. Franciscan Sister Sarah Kohles, OSF, reminds us that we toil in the church, with the church: "What does it mean to be in right relationship with the hierarchical structure of the Catholic Church?" We are invited to ask ourselves what it means to stay in our church. As the synod continues to unfold and yield a harvest that surprises at every stage, women religious need to engage with the hierarchical church prophetically. Sarah offers a creative framework to do this, to live into our name. She writes that we are called to the task of sistering the church: "I remain convinced that we transform the church by remaining in it. By insisting that something else is possible, refusing to leave, and taking up space and creating space for others, we transform the church from the inside."

Receding work tills the ground. The nutrients and oxygen will make the soil more fertile for the seeds the authors begin to name. Sister Monica Marie Cardona, VDMF, offers the image of "that tree rooted in the rocky clefts of the mountain and thriving against all odds, its roots have needed to grow longer." She explains the resiliency that such trees derive from their strong roots and small size. The ground we till is mountainous and windy, the place of change and inspiration for our church and world. Trusting our legacy, let us till this ground so God's abundance can do the rest!

Bibliography

Bowman, Thea. "Address to the U.S. Bishop's Conference." June 1989. https://www.usccb.org/issues-and-action/cultural-diversity/african-american/resources/upload/Transcript-Sr-Thea-Bowman-June-1989-Address.pdf.

Center for Applied Research in the Apostolate. *New Faces, New Possibilities: Cultural Diversity and Structural Change in Institutes of Women Religious*. Edited by Thomas P. Gaunt and Thu T. Do. Collegeville, MN: Liturgical Press, 2022.

Chima, Aneel, and Ron Gutman. "What It Takes to Lead through an Era of Exponential Change." *Harvard Business Review*. October 29, 2020. https://hbr.org/2020/10/what-it-takes-to-lead-through-an-era-of-exponential-change.

Clare of Assisi. "The Second Letter to Agnes of Prague." In *Clare of Assisi: Early Documents: The Lady*, edited by Regis J. Armstrong, 47–49. Hyde Park, NY: New City Press, 2006.

Dunn, Ted. "Refounding Religious Life: A Choice for Transformational Change." *Human Development* 30, no. 3 (Fall 2009).

Évole, Jordi, and Marius Sánchez, dirs. *The Pope: Answers*. 2003.

Farrell, Pat. "Navigating the Shifts." Presidential address presented at the Leadership Conference of Women Religious Assembly, 2012. https://www.lcwr.org/sites/default/files/news/files/pat_farrell_osf_-_lcwr_presidential_address_2012-_final.pdf.

Francis of Assisi, "Later Admonition and Exhortation to the Brothers and Sisters of Penance." In *Francis of Assisi: Early Documents: The Saint*, edited by Regis J. Armstrong, J. A. Wayne Hellmann, and William J. Short, 45–51. Hyde Park, NY: New City Press, 2001.

Francois, Susan Rose. "Inheriting Great Love and Responsibility." *Global Sisters Report*. March 20, 2015.

Francois, Susan Rose. "A Loving Gaze at Religious Life Realities. *Horizon* (Fall 2013).

Francois, Susan Rose. "Standing on the Shoulders of the Women Who Went Before Us." *Global Sisters Report*. August 10, 2023.

Gaffney, Evangelista. "Response to the Bishop's Questions." 1920.

Leadership Conference of Women Religious. "The Emerging Orientations: A Reflection." 2020. https://www.lcwr.org /files/page/files/the_emerging_orientations_of_lcwr_-_a _reflection.pdf.

Leadership Conference of Women Religious. "What We Are Seeing: An Analysis of Conversations about Religious Life as It Moves into the Future." February 2022. https://www .lcwr.org/files/pdf/what_we_are_seeing_02.22_0.pdf.

Lederach, John Paul. *The Moral Imagination: The Art and Soul of Building Peace*. New York: Oxford University Press, 2005.

"The Legend of Saint Clare." In *Clare of Assisi: Early Documents: The Lady*, edited by Regis J. Armstrong, 272–344. Hyde Park, NY: New City Press, 2006.

Lesher, Michelle. "Called to Revision Religious Life for the 21st Century." Presentation to the Sisters of St. Joseph of Peace Assembly, Spring 2023.

Lesher, Michelle. "Revisioning the Canonical Novitiate for the 21st Century." Doctoral dissertation, Fordham University, 2021.

Litz, Brett T., Nathan Stein, Eileen Delaney, Leslie Lebowitz, William P. Nash, Caroline Silva, and Shirq Maguen. "Moral Injury and Moral Repair in War Veterans: A Preliminary Model and Intervention Strategy." *Clinical Psychology Review*, vol. 29, no. 8 (December 2009): 695–706. http://doi.org/10.1016/j.cpr.2009.07.003.

Maya, Teresa. "Backwards to Move Forwards: History Matters in Formation." *InFormation*. Summer 2023.

Maya, Teresa. "Comunión 'En Salida': An Apostolic Call for Our Time in Religious Life." Presidential address presented at the Leadership Conference of Women Religious Assembly, 2018. https://www.lcwr.org/files/calendar/attachments /presidential_address_-_teresa_maya_ccvi.pdf.

Maya, Teresa. "An Open Letter to the Greatest Generation." *Global Sisters Report*. January 12, 2015.

Maya, Teresa. "USCCB Called to Communion." Address presented at the United States Conference of Catholic Bishops General Assembly, November 2018.

Mousel, Mary Eunice. *They Have Taken Root: The Sisters of the Third Order of St. Francis of the Holy Family*. New York: Bookman Associates, 1954.

Munley, Ann. "Learnings from the Collaborative Leadership Hubs." Presentation to the Leadership Conference of Women Religious Assembly, 2022. https://www.lcwr.org/files/pdf /2022_lcwr_assembly_-_learnings_from_the_collaborative _leadership_hubs.pdf.

Murray, Patricia. "Foreword." In *God's Call Is Everywhere: A Global Analysis of Contemporary Religious Vocations for Women*, vii–xvi. Collegeville, MN: Liturgical Press, 2023.

Nassif, Rosemary. "Supporting the Emergence of Global Sisterhood." Presentation to the Plenary Assembly of the International Union of Superiors General, Rome, Italy, May 2016. https://oldsite.uisg.org/meetings/assembly/.

National Religious Retirement Office. "Statistical Report." August 2023. https://www.usccb.org/resources/Statistical %20Report.pdf.

Park, Jung Eun Sophia. "Three Journeys to the Mystery." Keynote presentation to the Leadership Conference of Women Religious Assembly, 2023. https://lcwr.org/files /calendar/attachments/2023_lcwr_assembly_-_jung_eun _sophia_park_snjm.pdf.

Pasura, Dominic, and Marta Bivand Erdal. *Migration, Transnationalism and Catholicism: Global Perspectives*. London: Palgrave Macmillan, 2017.

Pellegrino, Mary. "Looking to the Future and Rooted in the Call." Presentation to Peace Ministries and the Sisters of St. Joseph of Peace, February 27, 2023.

Pope Francis. *Meeting with the Participants in the Fifth Convention of the Italian Church*. Vatican, November 15, 2015.

Pope Paul VI. *Perfectae Caritatis (Decree on the Adaptation and Renewal of Religious Life)*. Vatican, 1965.

Sheridan, William D. "Exponential Change Applies to Everything—Not Just Technology." *Business Learning Institute*. January 4, 2021. https://blionline.org/news/2172 -exponential-change-applies-to-everything-not-just -technology-2021-01-04.

Silf, Margaret. *The Other Side of Chaos: Breaking Through When Life Is Breaking Down*. Chicago: Loyola Press, 2011.

"The Sisters of Peace in the Diocese of Nottingham." *The Tablet*. January 12, 1884.

Sisters of St. Joseph of Peace. *Mother's Advice to Us from Her Deathbed*. 1920.

Sisters of St. Joseph of Peace. *Revised Tribute to Mother Evangelista*. 1965.

Sisters of St. Joseph of Peace. *Seeds of Peace: Acts of the 21st Congregation Chapter*. 2008.

Sisters of St. Joseph of Peace. *To Be Who We Say We Are: Acts of the 23rd Congregation Chapter*. 2022.

Stanco, Mary. "25th Jubilee Reflection." Homily given at jubilee liturgy of the Sisters of the Humility of Mary, July 15, 2023.

Swimme, Brian Thomas. "Cosmological Spirituality of Catholic Sisters." Keynote presentation to the Leadership Conference of Women Religious Assembly, 2023.

Tobin, Mary Luke. *Hope Is an Open Door: Journeys in Faith*. Nashville: Abingdon, 1981.

Trible, Phyllis. "Depatriarchalizing in Biblical Interpretation." *Journal of the American Academy of Religion* 41, no. 1 (March 1973): 30–48.

Vidulich, Dorothy. *Peace Pays a Price: A Study of Margaret Anna Cusack*. Englewood Cliffs, NJ: Kenmare Press, 2019.

Wilkins, Scout. "How Trees Grow in Rocks." May 19, 2018. https://travelinglight.life/how-trees-grow-in-rocks/.

World Health Organization. *International Classification of Diseases*, 11th Revision. Geneva: World Health Organization, 2018. https://icd.who.int/browse11/l-m/en.

Contributors

Chioma Ahanihu, SLW, is a Sister of the Living Word and has lived in Chicago since 2014. Born in Nigeria, she is currently the director of the Center for the Study of Consecrated Life at Catholic Theological Union, where she completed her doctorate in ministry degree.

Monica Marie Cardona, VDMF, originally from San Francisco, entered the Verbum Dei Missionary Fraternity in 2000. She made her final vows in 2008 and has since lived in Italy, Spain, and the United Kingdom, where she studied sacred scripture and worked in campus ministry. She is presently a councilor of the Verbum Dei general board in Rome.

Ricca Dimalibot, CCVI, professed perpetual vows in 2008. She is on the leadership team of the Sisters of Charity of the Incarnate Word, Houston. She is the medical director of CHRISTUS Point of Light Clinic, serving the uninsured and underserved.

Susan Rose Francois, CSJP, is a Sister of St. Joseph of Peace. She was a Bernardin Scholar at Catholic Theological Union and has served in congregation leadership since 2015. Susan is the author of *My Friend Joe: Reflections on St. Joseph* (2021).

Tracey Horan, SP, is a Sister of Providence of Saint Mary-of-the-Woods, Indiana. She entered the congregation in 2014 and professed final vows in 2022. She has ministered alongside migrant communities as a teacher and community organizer and currently lives and works at the United States–Mexico Border.

Katty Huanuco, CCVI, is a Sister of Charity of the Incarnate Word, San Antonio. She made her first vows in 2007. Katty shares her gifts with young religious life in the United States as part of Giving Voice's leadership core team, serves as a director at her congregation's social justice office, and is working on a PhD in social and public policy at Saint Louis University.

Nkechi Iwuoha, PHJC, serves on the leadership team of the American Province of the Poor Handmaids of Jesus Christ. She is on the LCWR board and a part-time adjunct professor in ethics in criminal justice and corrections at Calumet College of St. Joseph Whiting, Indiana. She made her first vows in Germany in 2004 and final vows in 2012.

Sarah Kohles, OSF, is an assistant professor of theology at Briar Cliff University in Sioux City, Iowa. She is an editor and contributor to *In Our Own Words: Religious Life in a Changing World* (2018) and *Creating Spaces for Women in the Catholic Church* (2023). She professed her final vows with the Sisters of St. Francis of Dubuque in 2011 and served on the Giving Voice Core Team.

Teresa Maya, CCVI, is a Sister of Charity of the Incarnate Word, San Antonio. She has a passion for the formation of ministers for Hispanics/Latinos in the United States. A native of Mexico, she has served in leadership in her community, the LCWR presidency, and is currently Senior Director of Sponsorship at the Catholic Health Association of the United States.

Juliet Mousseau, RSCJ, currently serves as the vice president for academic affairs at the Franciscan School of Theology in San Diego. Trained as a historical theologian, her writings include medieval theology, the history of her congregation, and contemporary questions in religious life. Her publications include *Prophetic Witnesses to Joy: A Theology of the Vowed Life* (2021).